ARCHITECTURE
ON THE CARPET

BRENDA AND ROBERT VALE

ARCHITECTURE
ON THE CARPET

The Curious Tale of Construction Toys
and the Genesis of Modern Buildings

with 111 illustrations, 97 in colour

Page 2: Arkitex Set B box lid (detail; see page 158 for full picture)

Publisher's note: *Architecture on the Carpet* is an independent publication and is not affiliated with, nor has it been authorized, sponsored, or otherwise approved by any of the toy manufacturers featured in the book. For more information on registered trade marks or patents, please contact the relevant intellectual property office.

First published in the United Kingdom in 2013 by
Thames & Hudson Ltd, 181A High Holborn, London WC1V 7QX

Copyright © 2013 Thames & Hudson Ltd, London

British Library Cataloguing-in-Publication Data
A catalogue record for this book is available from the British Library

ISBN 978-0-500-34285-5

Printed and bound in China by Everbest Printing Co. Ltd

To find out about all our publications, please visit
www.thamesandhudson.com.
There you can subscribe to our e-newsletter, browse or download
our current catalogue, and buy any titles that are in print.

CONTENTS

Toys
Are
Us

I F, ACCORDING TO WORDSWORTH, 'THE CHILD IS FATHER OF THE MAN'[1] does the construction toy therefore make the architect? If you played with Meccano (British but with many copies all over the world) do your buildings have a prefabricated engineered appearance with lots of holes in bits of the structure? If you played with Girder and Panel (American but with a British copy) are your buildings typical of so much commercial architecture, high-rise blocks with frames clad with panels of glass and sometimes solid material?

In the middle of the nineteenth century a group of architects emphasized the importance of the learning environment to a child's development, stating that what was experienced then would be 'carried to the end of life'.[2] Designers of educational toys from Friedrich Froebel with his famous blocks[3] to Hilary Page, an early user of plastic for toys and a man who could have claimed to have invented Lego,[4] have also built reputations on the idea that their toys would form the mind of the child in the best possible way. This book tries to look for similarities between what you can build with a selection of construction toys and the architecture that these seem to represent best, as well as being an excuse to have a lot of fun playing with them.

The toy industry is international. Just as modern architecture spread from the beginning of the twentieth century to become almost an instrument of globalization, so toys could also claim to be a unifying factor in the spread of ideas.

Germany started the trend with the successful Richter's Blocks, but American Lincoln Logs and their many imitators have also ensured children around the world can build log cabins on the carpet, and even good old British Meccano was made under licence as far away as Argentina. While it is of course not quite true that the whole course of modern architecture was set by the construction toys of the modern period, as early as the 1920s Bilt-E-Z, an American metal toy, could be used to construct the iconic stepped-back skyscraper,[5] just like the 1931 McGraw Hill and Empire State buildings in New York. Later, the British Arkitex mirrored the steel-framed glass towers and office blocks of the modern era.

Not all construction toys looked forward to (or even sideways at) change in the built environment. Richter's Blocks never really progressed beyond building a mythical image of medieval Germany, in America Lincoln Logs perpetuated the legend of the frontier and Wild West in its many versions of miniature log cabins, and in Britain black-and-white Tudor Minibrix were sold with a grainy photograph of seventeenth-century houses in the village of Weobley in Herefordshire, so redolent of 'olde England'.

The toys featured in this book are only a few examples of the very many different building toys that have been sold in the last hundred or so years. There are families among these toys, such as those that stack, like Richter's Blocks, those with interlocking bricks, like modern Lego, and those with systems that bear no resemblance to how buildings are really put together, like Bayko. We have tried to pick examples of different types of construction systems, as well as toys that seem, at least to us, to have a relationship with architecture. Some excellent ones never made these pages: the 1930s French toy Assemblo made Bilt-E-Z-like stepped-back towers from metal plates that were joined by thread-ing rods through their intersecting edges; the 1940–50 DuPage Vinylite Plastic Building Sets from Chicago made very good small, modern, flat-roofed houses that seem to have stepped straight from the pages of contemporary issues of *Architectural Forum* (although this was probably because the smaller sets did not come with the more expensive pitched roofs); for real Art Deco fantasies it is hard to beat the 1930s British printed-paper construction toy Samlo; and in wonderful miniature there was the 1960s Merit Toddlers Towers [sic], which stacked up to make tiny tower blocks. We hope you may be inspired to track these down and have a go with them and with the ones we feature. The great thing about architecture on the carpet is that it is so easy to have another try if your building turns out a total mess.

CHAPTER ONE

Modernism on the Line

W HILE THIS BOOK EXPLORES MAINLY the link between construction toys and architecture, we begin by looking at toy train sets
and the modernist designs they introduced to the families who
played with them. Toy trains were invented by Märklin in Germany,[1] refined
in America by Joshua Lionel Cowen (of Lionel trains)[2] and hugely popular in
Britain, but it is not so much the trains that we will be discussing, as the stations
they stopped at.

The world's first public railway, the Stockton and Darlington Railway in
northern England, opened in 1825 with a 26 mile (42 km)-long track; by 1860
there were over 10,000 miles (16,000 km) of track.[3] In the United States by the
same date there were around 30,000 miles (48,000 km) of track. It is hardly surprising that fairly soon there were toy trains, which initially were either pushed
along the floor or ran across it powered by clockwork or, with more potential for
harm to the carpet, steam.[4] However, model railways as a system came when the
German firm Märklin demonstrated their first complete clockwork railway
system in 1891.[5] Originally Märklin had manufactured metal kitchen utensils,
and their first toys were miniature versions of these for dolls' houses.[6] They
quickly realized this was an excellent way of creating continuing sales, as once a
child (well, probably a girl) had a dolls' house it could then be added to with
additional furniture and fittings *ad infinitum*. With toy railways they followed the

same path, making not only locomotives, but carriages, goods wagons, rails, points, crossings, turntables, signals and, of course, stations. In both cases they created the idea of a system of parts, so that having bought the initial dolls' house or train set, you could carry on adding to it to make a larger and larger system, with parts that fitted together to work as a whole. The Germans in fact started the whole idea of toys as an expandable system, not just with trains, but also with building blocks, as we shall see later.[7]

As part of this total train system there had to be stations. By the early 1900s the German manufacturers offered a magnificent range of stations and accessories for them (including lamps, bells, ticket machines, cattle pens and telegraphs) for both the wealthy buyer and the (relatively) poor.[8] The British were happy to buy German toy trains, but real trains look quite different from country to country, so the German manufacturers took to making models that looked vaguely British or American in outline and were painted in the liveries of the big railway companies.[9]

When the Germans became the enemy in 1914 it was no longer acceptable for patriotic Britons to import German toys, and British manufacturers began to make train sets. At least they did once the war was over and they were no longer busy manufacturing armaments. One of these manufacturers was Frank Hornby, who, at the beginning of the twentieth century, had invented a toy made of metal strips, wheels and other parts that could be bolted together to make a whole variety of mechanical toys. He marketed this as Mechanics Made Easy, but it became much better known under its new name of Meccano (see Chapter 3). With wonderful self-confidence, Frank Hornby called his new trains not Meccano Trains but Hornby Trains, and they soon developed a life of their own as part of the expanding Meccano empire based in Liverpool.[10]

Stations come at hugely different scales, needing a hierarchy of treatments from the halt to the terminus, yet all having to be a practical interface between the traveller and the train. Big stations have long been an unhappy marriage between an imposing or fancy front, often incorporating a hotel, for the people and the large engineered shed at the back for the trains. However, the grand termini, which were in part used as flagships to represent the company running the railway line,[11] have not been a major feature of toy train sets, since it is hard to reconcile the scale (or indeed the dead end) with the circle or oval of track that forms the starting point of most toy trains. In the main, toy stations have been modest rural archetypes that sit to one side of the line, or two-platform suburban models with a double track running through the middle for those with more money, space or ambition.

An important question for makers of toy railways was: what should the buildings look like? It has been suggested that few people pause to look at the architecture of railway stations, 'if they are pausing it is to curse a missed train or to join a queue to catch the next one.'[12] With a toy station, you see the structure whenever you play with the trains. Whereas the engineering and glass construction of the great 'train shed' over the platforms is most magnificent when seen from within, models are normally seen from above. The toy station therefore needs to have sufficient detail to make it externally attractive when looking down on it. The small nineteenth-century station provided that, and there were plenty around to provide prototypes. (In 1901, when the death of Queen Victoria ended the Victorian era, almost the whole of the British railway system was already in existence,[13] so all British railway stations were, in practice, Victorian.) For many years the need to provide somewhere for passengers to await the train in shelter and for the railway staff to conduct the business of running a railway, including the selling of tickets, happened most often in small buildings with domestic comforts, even to the extent of maintaining a station garden. The epitome of this approach is Wolferton Station in Norfolk, which was built in 1862, the same year that Queen Victoria purchased the nearby Sandringham Estate; the royal connection led the station to be known as Sandringham Station. The question for those designing toy train sets was whether stations should look picturesquely rural, like Sandringham, or emphatically modern, like Surbiton in Surrey (see page 17), the place where Harry chats up a girl in the refreshment room in the film of *Harry Potter and the Half-Blood Prince*.

Initially the manufacturers made stations that represented what the travelling public might see when they boarded a train. Märklin, Hornby, Lionel, American Flyer,[14] and their competitors, reflected the nineteenth-century nature of the railway and its architecture in lithographed tinplate. However, for British model railway owners this was soon to change, thanks to Wenman Joseph Bassett-Lowke. Born in Northampton in 1877, he left school at thirteen and, after working for eighteen months in an architect's office, he went into his father's boiler-making business. As a hobby he began making model steam engines, and soon founded a mail-order market for model engine components.[15]

Now privately owned, the station at Wolferton, Norfolk, was where royalty
and their guests arrived to stay at nearby Sandringham House.

Following a visit to the Paris Fair of 1900 where the German manufacturers of model railways made a deep impression, Bassett-Lowke began to import steam-driven British-styled models from Germany, working with the British model railway enthusiast Henry Greenly. The first Bassett-Lowke model shop opened in London in 1908 and moved to 112 High Holborn in 1910, where its close neighbour was the new London tourist office of the city of Blackpool. Blackpool Corporation commissioned Bassett-Lowke to make display models of the Blackpool Tower and the Big Wheel to put in the window to attract tourists, and so Bassett-Lowke suggested that E. W. Twining, who made model flying machines that Bassett-Lowke also sold, should become the firm's architectural model maker.

Through his shops, his mail-order business, and his work with toy manufacturers, Bassett-Lowke was to play an influential part in the world of models and construction toys in Britain until the 1950s. He was also, significantly, a pioneering patron of avant-garde architecture. His first commission (in 1916) was for the conversion and extension of a small terraced house at 78 Derngate, Northampton, where he planned to live after getting married. His first choice of architect was Alexander Anderson, a Northampton-based Scot.[16] However, Bassett-Lowke then engaged a much more famous Scottish architect, Charles Rennie Mackintosh, to carry out the work; this was to be Mackintosh's first building outside Scotland. The alterations to the street façade were modest, but the garden façade was remodelled into a dramatic white elevation that has been described as pre-dating any other modern movement work in Great Britain.[17] The interiors were also remodelled and extensively and strikingly redecorated with panelling and stencilled patterns. The whole house also had new Mackintosh furniture and the overall design has been described as the start of a new phase in Mackintosh's career.[18] The striped decoration he designed for the walls and ceiling of the guest bedroom was considered so shocking that when the playwright George Bernard Shaw stayed with the Bassett-Lowkes in 1923, he was asked if it disturbed him: 'No,' he replied, 'I always sleep with my eyes closed.'[19]

In 1923 Bassett-Lowke commissioned the German architect Peter Behrens to design a new, bigger, house on the Wellingborough Road in Northampton.[20] Behrens, arguably the first industrial designer in the modern sense, had begun working for Allgemeine Elektrizitäts Gesellschaft (AEG) in 1907, designing a whole range of products from light fittings and electric kettles to factory buildings. In 1909 he had designed the huge Turbinenfabrik in Berlin for the manufacture of turbine generators;[21] this was described by Le Corbusier, who worked for Behrens for five months in 1910, as a 'Cathedral of Work'.[22] Behrens was a key member of the Deutscher Werkbund, formed in 1907 by artists, designers, industrialists and architects to promote modern, integrated design.[23] Bassett-Lowke was a member of the Design and Industries Association (DIA), the UK equivalent of the Deutscher Werkbund, and had made contact with members of the Werkbund before 1914, through his association with the German toymaker Stefan Bing. It has been suggested that he chose Behrens after looking at illustrations of his work for AEG in the 1913 Werkbund catalogue.[24]

The house that Behrens designed for Bassett-Lowke was, according to one commentator, the first 'international modern' movement house to be built in England.[25] It was completed in 1926 and was traditional in plan, with a symmetrical two-storey arrangement. Both main façades are symmetrical, and show that Behrens had quite a good grasp of the principles of passive solar design: the north-facing street façade had few windows and no first-floor glazing, apart from a projecting triangular vertical strip to light the landing, while the sunny southern garden façade had large windows and balconies. By the 1920s Behrens was no longer a young radical, and in architectural terms the house, built from white-painted rendered brickwork, is more Art Deco than modern, but even now it appears quite shocking compared with its traditional neighbours.[26]

As well as commissioning houses, Bassett-Lowke was also busy with model railways. In 1922 he and Henry Greenly, perhaps conscious that many households in Britain's growing suburbs were not spacious, ordered a series of train sets from Bing in Germany that were half the size of the, until then, smallest O Gauge. This 'OO Gauge' system was called the Bing Table Top Railway, and while crude it was both cheap and comprehensive, with electric and clockwork locomotives, track and points, and a range of buildings and accessories. Unfortunately, it was not a great success.[27]

However, in the 1930s Bing and his German partners formed a new company called Trix, which began by making metal construction sets, a little like Meccano but with more holes. Bassett-Lowke persuaded them to have another try at the OO Gauge and the result was an electric railway system called Trix Express, which was sold in England as the Trix Twin Railway. It was called Twin because its novel feature was the use of a three-rail track, on a Bakelite base, which allowed the locomotive to be set to pick up power from the rail on either one side or the other, so that two trains could be run under independent control on the same track. This of course allowed for exciting collisions.

The Trix Twin system was soon being manufactured in England with two remarkably unrealistic locomotives, comprising a small four-wheeled tank engine and a small four-wheeled tender engine, painted in the liveries of the 'Big Four' railway companies. (Britain's private railway companies were formed into four large companies in an act of semi-nationalization in 1923. These were the London, Midland and Scottish Railway [LMS]; the Great Western Railway [GWR]; the London and North Eastern Railway [LNER] and the Southern Railway [SR]).[28] Assorted coaches and goods wagons were made to go with the locomotives. In addition to the rolling stock, Trix Twin offered an elaborate range of station buildings, initially in wood and then in die-cast metal. These were designed by Bassett-Lowke's model maker E. W. Twining[29] and were in a determinedly modernist style.

Most British railway companies either ignored modernism (the Great Western Railway had been built by the great Victorian engineer Isambard Kingdom Brunel, and probably did not feel the need to improve its image), or did not have a building programme that allowed them to exploit this approach. Both the LMS and the LNER put their modern image work into the design of streamlined express locomotives for their London–Scotland services. The GWR did put some streamlining onto its engine *King Henry VII*, but it looked like a token gesture, although they made some very smart streamlined diesel railcars.[30] However, the LMS did build a couple of modern hotels. The double-glazed Queen's Hotel in Leeds (1937) was designed by the architects of the Dorchester in London, William Hamlyn and William Curtiss Green.[31] Of greater significance was the same company's Midland Hotel (1933) in Morecambe, designed by Oliver Hill. This is an elegant white three-storey curved building opposite the railway station, right on the seafront. It had murals by Eric Ravilious and Eric Gill, who also provided some sculpture, and textiles by Marion Dorn.[32]

However, a notable promoter of modernism was the Southern Railway; all the stations on the last line it constructed in 1939, the Chessington branch, were in the modernist style.[33] The precedent for this approach was the much larger station at Surbiton (1937), which was designed by Southern Railway's Architects' Department under J. R. Scott to replace an existing station.

'New Ways', Bassett-Lowke's modernist house in Northampton, was designed by
German architect Peter Behrens in 1926.

Surbiton Station, designed by the Southern Railway Architects' Department, was opened in 1937.

The 1932 Arnos Grove Underground Station with its circular booking hall was designed by Charles Holden, the architect of many modernist Underground stations.

Surbiton is a large building of white-painted reinforced concrete with a flat roof and a clock tower, and contains a booking office as well as kiosks and shops.[34] Its modern style may have been seen as a reflection of the modernization process that occurred when the entire Southern Railway suburban system and some of its mainlines were electrified in the 1930s. There may already have been a Southern predilection for concrete, as the company owned a precast concrete plant in Exmouth, where it made fences, signs and footbridges.[35]

The most famous patron of modern railway architecture between the two world wars was the Underground Electric Railways Company of London, which became part of the London Passenger Transport Board in 1933. Its chief executive officer Frank Pick was another founder member of the DIA, along with the architect Charles Holden. Indeed, the influence of the DIA is seen strongly in this whole history of railway modernism; Pick is quoted as saying in 1925 '…we are going to build our stations…to the most modern pattern…. We are going to represent the DIA gone mad, and in order that I may go mad in good company I have got Holden to see that we do it properly.'[36] The increasingly austere modern buildings that Pick commissioned from Holden have been described as 'some of the finest English architecture…of this century,'[37] and certainly count as railway architecture, even if they were not built for a 'proper' railway, but for the Underground. In fact the Underground inspired very few toy trains, although Hornby did launch a model of one of the Metropolitan Railway's electric locomotives in 1925. Initially this ran on mains voltage, which made for exciting health and safety issues in the playroom.

When Bassett-Lowke produced modernist station buildings, they reflected the idea that the railways represented progress and the future. The analogy now might be with France's Trains à Grande Vitesse (TGV), or China's CRH (China Railway High-speed) network. In both countries the new trains and their dramatic new stations have become an important part of national identity. The house Behrens designed for Bassett-Lowke was called 'New Ways' and the Trix station system was called, perhaps in homage to it, 'Many Ways'. The modern station was represented in a clever series of interchangeable components that could create anything from a rural halt to a large terminus. Unlike its buildings, Trix Twin locomotives were not modern-looking. Its initial offerings were toy-like four-wheeled engines, quite unlike anything seen in reality, although these were joined by a streamlined, incredibly expensive Coronation Scot just before the outbreak of the Second World War (which event put a stop to Trix Twin

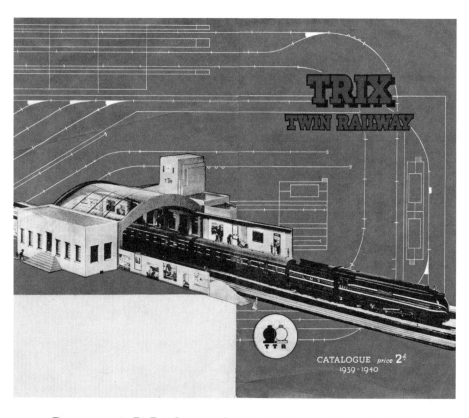

The very expensive Trix Twin Coronation Scot departing from a modular, modernist-style Trix Many Ways station.

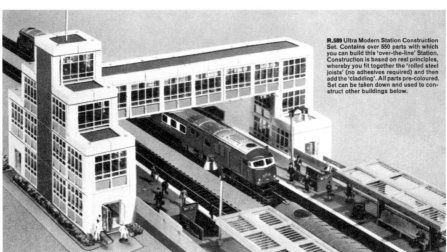

R.589 Ultra Modern Station Construction
Set. Contains over 550 parts with which
you can build this 'over-the-line' Station.
Construction is based on real principles,
whereby you fit together the 'rolled steel
joists' (no adhesives required) and then
add the 'cladding'. All parts pre-coloured.
Set can be taken down and used to construct other buildings below.

(Top) One of the first Hornby Dublo trains, the 1939 streamlined A4 Pacific express
locomotive, surrounded by Dinky Toys vehicles, also made by Meccano.

(Above) A Tri-ang model Blue Pullman departing from the 1966 Tri-ang 'ultra-modern'
station made of Arkitex parts.

production for the duration). Trix Twin also made a rather crude Southern electric train, so you could have a miniature model of Surbiton in all the glory of both architecture and rolling stock.

Hornby, makers only of O gauge trains, soon realized that Trix Twin would eat into their sales, and came up with a completely new system called Hornby Dublo (ie 'double O' or OO gauge). This was available initially in clockwork and electric versions, and started with a tank engine, in four different liveries, for suburban and goods trains, and a streamlined LNER A4 Pacific for expresses, plus suitable coaches and wagons.

Right from the start the Hornby trains, unlike Trix Twin, were fairly accurate replicas of real locomotives, were cheaper, and ran on 12 volts DC rather than Trix's 15 volts AC. The big advantage of DC was that the train could be reversed by turning the controller handle in the other direction, while to reverse a Trix Twin train required a break in the current which switched a relay in the cab and reversed the contacts to the motor. This was all very well, but tended to happen unexpectedly owing to dirty track and other problems, leading to a certain amount of unintentional reversing, which did little to help the appearance of realism. Realism in Trix Twin was not helped either by the brass caps sticking out of the side of the engine, which gave access to the brushes of the electric motor. Hornby avoided all this by using DC, and managed to get all the 'works' hidden inside the locomotive, making for a much more convincing model. Their big streamlined express locomotive even provided a realistic representation of the Walschaerts valve gear (found on many steam engines). Hornby advertising made much of this feature.

So Hornby had the modern streamlined locomotive, and to go with it they copied Trix and offered a series of modern streamlined buildings. At first these were made of wood with the windows painted on and the cynic might suggest that their design was modernist because this style was easier to achieve in painted wooden blocks. However, after the war the wooden buildings were replaced by cast metal ones, more like those of Trix, and these continued to give an impression of concrete construction, although Hornby's buildings were complete objects rather than Trix's systematized set of flexible components.

After the war a third British manufacturer joined the fray. This was the well-known toy company Tri-ang. Trix Twin and Hornby Dublo locomotives were made of cast metal, with the rolling stock of tin-printed sheet steel. Tri-ang right from the start used modern materials – plastics – for locomotives, rolling stock and even track, with just the rails in metal. This made Tri-ang trains both more realistic – the track had only two rails rather than three – and quite cheap. The first plastic they used was cellulose acetate, which is prone to distortion over time and means that many early Tri-ang trains are now nothing like the shape they were supposed to be. Their stations were formed from a series of flexible components, like Trix's Many Ways but in plastic, and they made not modern but rather typically nineteenth-century buildings. However, Tri-ang did espouse modernism in the 1960s, and changed their station design to something that reflected the new, and architecturally slightly depressing, image of British Railways, to go with models of the latest diesel locomotives and the streamlined Blue Pullman that was perhaps Britain's first modern train. Eventually Tri-ang even produced an 'ultra-modern station' using the building set Arkitex, which was made by another part of the Tri-ang empire (see Chapter 12).

Both pre-war British purveyors of model railways – Trix Twin and Hornby – offered exclusively modern buildings. This would have exposed the buyers, children and, no doubt, their fathers (who often appeared in the catalogues playing an enthusiastic part in the proceedings) to architecture that they would not be likely to see as railway passengers. This is almost entirely due to Bassett-Lowke. Perhaps this is a more important influence on attitudes to design than has been acknowledged, and could be seen as one of the biggest successes of the Design and Industries Association. After all, if you travelled on the London Underground, or on the Southern Railway, you got modern design more or less as a by-product of your trip, but if you bought a Many Ways or Hornby Dublo station you were actively choosing the modern. It certainly shows a significant link between toys and architecture.

CHAPTER TWO

Richter's Blocks and the Castles on the Rhine

ICHTER'S BLOCKS, OR ANKER-STEINBAUKASTEN (Anchor Stone
Building Sets), are almost as far from modernism as you can go. These
exquisite blocks that always leave you smelling slightly of linseed oil are
shaped and coloured in such a way as to satisfy every Gothic fancy you have ever
had when it comes to buildings. They are the ideal medium for making a miniature hideaway for a Sleeping Beauty or one of Tolkien's *Two Towers*. The blocks
first appeared in 1880 and are still manufactured today,[1] making the toy a long-
lasting German achievement. In part this is due to Richter's original promotion
of the product, but it also has much to do with the buildings you can make with
the stacked blocks. Richter's Blocks form one of the lesser-known triumphs of
German industrialization. This might also owe something to the German
concept of *Heimat* (very roughly: homeland, or belonging to a homeland), since
what the toy builds best is an idealized version of the Germany of myth and
legend, but the blocks were also an export success, perhaps because of this very
link with fantasy and fairy story.

Designed to look like stone, the blocks are a mixture of chalk, sand, and
colouring in a linseed oil varnish matrix. This means they are self-coloured (in
cream, red and blue) rather then painted, and they are heavier than a wooden
brick of corresponding size, so more stable when stacked high. The material was
invented in 1875 by Gustav Lilienthal, an artist who designed toys, and his

The smallest set of Richter's Blocks came with a rather morbid set of suggestions for making gravestones.

brother Otto, who is far better known as a pioneer aviator. The Lilienthals were not successful in promoting the product and eventually sold their patent to the German chemical industrialist, Friedrich Richter. Alongside his pharmaceutical factory in Rudolstadt Richter built a factory for the production of the toy blocks with an art department where artists produced the designs and plans that went with the sets. Richter created the first systematic set of building toys: you could start with a small set and add extensions to make larger sets as you progressed.

Unlike the Lilienthals, Richter understood marketing, exhibiting the sets at various fairs. He also realized that a product that appealed to adults as well would be more likely to be a success. Consequently special sets were produced that made large and complex structures, as well as those with simpler instructions for children to follow.[2] Architect Walter Gropius was said to be fascinated by the toy,[3] which is, perhaps, surprising, since Richter's blocks, with their arches, pinnacles and diamond-tiled roofs, seem to be designed for German medieval buildings, especially castles, rather than the modernist geometry of Gropius' Bauhaus school. Richter's own villa in Rudolstat looks as if it could be made of the stone blocks (which in a sense it was, as damaged toy blocks were used as landfill on the site in 1890).[4]

Hundreds of thousands of sets of Richter's Blocks have been sold worldwide, with early exports to the UK, Holland and the US. Publicity for the construction toy came with Richter's building of large and detailed models for various exhibitions, starting with the Great Castle of 1884 for the Antwerp Universal Exhibition. Many of these exhibition models were of castles and churches, both building types that seem particularly suited to the stone effect of Richter's Blocks.

The blocks came in three basic colours: cream, terracotta and blue. However, the range of types was vast. In the original series of 1884, GK AF (Grosskaliber Steine Alte Folge – large calibre stones, old series), there were 359 different block types.[5] A new series (GK NF or Grosskaliber Steine Neue [new] Folge) appeared ten years later. There were also special blocks and roof tiles and iron parts, the latter especially for making bridges, so that a total collection of parts could run to over a thousand pieces. Nevertheless, the sets started very small. Set 0, the first set in the GK NF series of 1894, consisted of only nineteen blocks of ten types.[6] Rather gloomily, the first models you are encouraged to make are a series of gravestones in leafy cemetery settings. Even more instructions for increasingly elaborate gravestones are found in the larger Set 2.

Gateways were popular early models; those with crosses on top were presumably entrances to the cemeteries. In the late-nineteenth-century sets there are plans for small churches alongside the larger gateways and memorials, and by Set 12 a whole series of plans for buildings and bridges are offered, including a rather Germanic Chinese Fort. Only after the Second World War, when the factory at Rudolstadt became part of East Germany, did the smallest sets make models that might be thought more appropriate for children, such as a lorry, a train without wheels, and various small buildings with pitched roofs.[7] Since the sets could be built up gradually over a series of birthdays, Christmases and visiting uncles, a middle-class family could finish with a collection of the multi-coloured blocks capable of building substantial castles and churches, such as those found along the Rhine.

One such castle is the Mäuseturm (Mouse Tower), a toll tower built (according to legend) in the tenth century by the Archbishops of Mainz, which gained fame in the first half of the nineteenth century through August Kopisch's poem *Der Mäuseturm*,[8] and Robert Southey's *God's Judgement on a Wicked Bishop*.[9] Both poems concern the fate of Bishop Hatto, who burned starving peasants to death, thereby ridding the area of what he described as 'vermin', rather than sharing his granary full of grain. The next morning his servants reported that all the grain had been eaten by mice (or rats, depending on the version of the story) who were now in pursuit of the Bishop. Although Hatto retreated to what he thought was a safe fortress, the toll tower in the middle of the Rhine, the mice swam across and eventually drove him mad, or devoured him, or both. This is just one of many legends related to the Rhine that appear to turn recorded history on its head, since Archbishop Hatto of Mainz has been described as an able ruler who brought prosperity to the city.[10]

The picturesque Mouse Tower looks as if could be constructed in life-size Richter's Blocks (and plans exist for making a similar toy tower[11]). It was one of around forty medieval castles built along the Rhine, many of which were destroyed in the seventeenth century when France and Germany were battling for supremacy. Fighting ceased in 1814 when Prussia became the ruler of the whole middle Rhine area;[12] in addition, river tolls were abolished in 1868, allowing the opening up of trade – one key to the success of German industrialization. At the same time this industrialization, as elsewhere in the world, brought with it a sense of troubling change, of old against new.[13] It is less than surprising, perhaps, that Richter's Blocks and the fantasy castles and buildings they made

The Mouse Tower in the middle of the Rhine, where Bishop Hatto was believed
to have come to a sticky end.

were such a success, because they reconciled this opposition. They represented simultaneously the new Germany and the Germany of history and legends – the essence of Germany, or *Heimat*. The new German middle class could thus be ideally German by believing in this idea of *Heimat* while living and behaving in a modern industrialized culture,[14] and Richter's Blocks ensured these German ideals were instilled in their children on the nursery carpet.

The successes of nineteenth-century industrialization in both Germany and Britain caused unease,[15] but in Britain in particular it led to despondency related to doubt about those very successes. In Britain, for example, new phenomena such as the railways were feared: Dickens's reference in *Pickwick Papers*, amid a list of the horrors of travelling, to 'boilers bursting' is hardly reassuring,[16] while the Duke of Wellington was troubled that the new railways would allow the lower classes to move much more freely, possibly leading to revolution.[17] In contrast, in Germany Berthold Auerbach describes an 'idyll on the railway' as a marriage between the new railway in the valley and the old castle on the hill, with the house of the railway linesman framed in oak with flowers blooming on the wooden balcony.[18]

This ability to see the railway not as a threat to an essentially natural, rural and predictable way of life but as a picturesque part of the natural world has its counterpart in the ethos of Richter's Blocks. Although they came late to railways (plans for stations did not appear until 1923 and were more modern in character in a deliberate effort to update the style of their buildings[19]) Richter's Blocks can be seen to reflect the way Germany managed to combine an attachment to a romantic, mythical past with an embrace of the challenges of modern industrialization. Here was a product made in a factory and heavily marketed, true to the industrial capitalist ideal, but which made small structures suggestive of another world. At the same time some of the Rhine castles whose forms it could be used to imitate, and most of which were now in a ruinous state, were being bought up and converted into summer residences by the new wealthy industrialists.

The original medieval castles of the Rhine were military buildings, each essentially a stronghold where the aristocratic owner and his family could be safe, where his subjects could shelter in times of attack, and from which his own armed forces could emerge to attack others. Situated on high ground for practical rather than romantic reasons, they were constructed and rebuilt pragmatically rather than to embody medieval aesthetic principles or the world of chivalry.

However, at the time Richter's Blocks appeared, historic ruined castles were being recreated to fit in with an imagined medieval past; this was like playing with the building sets, but it was model-castle building on a 1:1 scale.

Many ruined strongholds and castles were saved from further destruction and converted into living space, which raises the question as to whether the act of saving buildings rewrites history. The critic John Ruskin contended it was more 'honest' when old structures were left to show their age, and hence their true history, since like the dead it was impossible to resurrect an old building through its restoration.[20] But arguably the repair of old buildings to extend their useful life can be part of their history, even if modern materials are used. Nevertheless, converting part of a castle to a modern hotel in the name of conservation (such as happened to the thirteenth-century Liebenstein Castle, or the fourteenth-century Katz Castle, both in the middle of the Rhine valley) hardly gives the weary traveller an authentic medieval experience. At least the Richter's Block castle remains true to its type.

Those who could afford to convert castles tended to be royalty. One of the great castles on the Rhine, Stolzenfels Palace,[21] was a ruin when in 1823 it was given by the city of Koblenz to Crown Prince Frederick, who had declared his wish to own a Rhine castle, having been stunned by the beauty of the Rhine Gorge after his first trip along the river in 1815.[22] It is always useful to do service to a Prussian Prince and future King, although the city may also have seen that having royalty living nearby would attract tourists, as the castle still does.[23] The conversion work also gave employment to local craftsmen. The main plan for the conversion was drawn up by the German neoclassical architect Karl Friedrich Schinkel, who was also at home with the Gothic Revival style, as seen at Stolzenfels, because of his architectural work in the preservation of some of Germany's other historic buildings.[24] The castle, with its castellations and yellow plastered walls, formed a model for how other ruined Rhine castles could be converted into places to live, or at least stay for a short time.[25]

The picturesque ruins of the nearby Lahneck Castle[26] were also rebuilt, from the middle of the century onwards, in Gothic style.[27] As at Stolzenfels, flat roofs and crenellations became features of the conversion. Pitched roofs were a later twentieth-century addition. The final form, however, reflects the young Goethe's 1774 observation that the tower of ruined Lahneck was a place where the ghosts of noble heroes would rest. These notions were later included in his poem 'Geistesgruss'.[28]

This conservation of ruins was thus, at the same time, the regeneration of history through the preservation and of changes to the ruins themselves, and the recreation of the history of Germany. It is hardly surprising, therefore, that the early designs for Richter's blocks were focussed on such building types as castles and Gothic churches.

The Rhine castles were the gateway to the world of myth and legend. As they did with Goethe, these medieval buildings and ruins inspired poets, novelists and painters pursuing the picturesque and the sublime. As early as 1802, poet and philosopher Friedrich Schlegel had praised the Rhine Valley for being rough and wild, and hence a beautiful landscape.[29] Such landscapes are also the inspiration for 'Gothic' tales, such as that of the Lorelei; she is supposed to sit on an echoing rock in the middle of the Rhine, combing her hair and, with the beauty of her singing, lure sailors to their death in the treacherous river. The various versions of her story were distilled in Heinrich Heine's 1823 poem *Die Lorelei*.[30] The constant remaking of the legend led Victor Hugo to comment, when he visited the rock and found its famous echo was not as echoing as he had been led to believe, that 'It is probable that the Oreade (mountain nymph) of Lurley [sic], formerly courted by so many princes and mythological counts, begins to get hoarse and fatigued.'[31] However, so important was this myth to the German sense of identity that Heine's poem remained in print under the Nazis, despite Heine's Jewish ancestry, although it was attributed to an unknown writer.[32] This reverence for the story in its many versions helped to reinforce the poem as the telling of a folk myth rather than the product of the drawing room.

From *Die Lorelei* it is a short step to Wagner and his ladies of the Rhine. Charged with looking after the Rhine gold, his Rhine Maidens appear at the start and end of the Ring Cycle. Although most of the myths of Wagner's operas have a Norse origin,[33] the composer used these and his knowledge of the German countryside to create realistic but definitely German settings for his operas.[34] Some of these were performed against backdrops of medieval castles, such as those by scene painters Heinrich Döll[35] and Christian Jank.[36] The latter also provided early sketches for Neuschwanstein Castle, the fantastical embodiment by King Ludwig of Bavaria of a wealth of fictional ideas about the past. Ludwig originally planned to recreate the mythical world of his friend Wagner in his dream 'robber baron' castle, which was started in 1868 but still not finished by the time of Ludwig's death in 1886.[37]

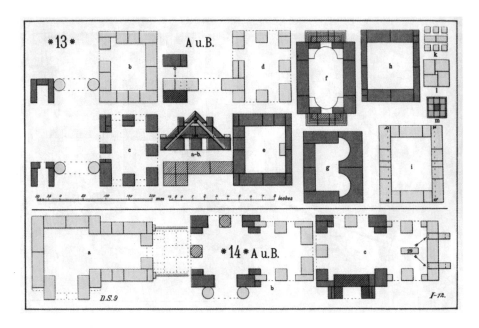

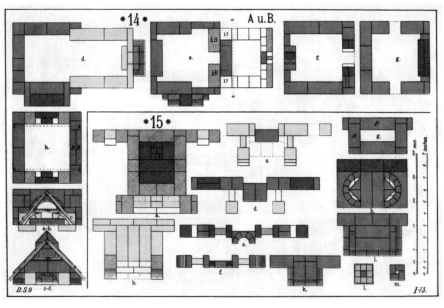

Instructions for making the Town Watch House, showing how the blocks were to be set out.

A

B

D.S.9.

14.

Thus castles are intimately linked not just with the history of the Rhine but with a history of Germany created in the name of art, and a rather patriotic art at that. With this background, the castles of the Rhine were treasured for all that they represented – and if you could not afford a castle a set of Richter's Blocks was a plausible substitute.

Unlike other construction toys discussed in this book, the Richter models were often set in an imaginary context. Normally this was an illustration of the finished model with the implied scale given by the size of the figures drawn alongside. A plan view is usually given in a separate book. The context is used to reinforce the imagery in the picture, such as the medieval figures in front of the Watch House. However, the context is more important than a realistic view of each side of the building, as seen opposite, where weather vane and flag indicate that the wind direction reverses from one side of the building to the other.

Supporting the imagination by supplying the context in this way reinforces the creation of the ideal homeland or *Heimat*. As part of this, greenery and especially trees are an important part of most settings. Forests were as much part of the ideal romantic landscape as were rocks, gorges and castles, but there was at the time a fear that industrialization was threatening the very forests that such writers as Wilhelm Riehl (in his 1851 *Natural History of the German People*) saw as part of German culture and hence *Heimat*.[38] In the Richter illustrations, trees, like people, are used to give scale, normally making the buildings appear much larger than might be imagined from their details. In fact the early sets came with paper trees, people and bushes to be cut out and positioned around the constructed models. These additions seem as unnecessary as the paper clock faces and Gothic windows that could be pasted onto the finished model, but which destroyed the essential flexibility of the toy as a whole.

The Richter world is a fantasy world, depicting ideal German models in ideal settings, and all that is required are a set of bricks, a flat surface and imagination. Germany is not an island and the borders of the German-speaking peoples have been in a state of change over many years; as a consequence a specifically German identity had been hard to define. Germany had to identify itself as a nation at the point when industrialization clamoured for national unity and the creation of a national market, and when local traditions began to disappear. Historian and German scholar Peter Blickle suggests that this period in Germany led to the creation of *Heimat* as a fusion of self, landscape, nature and identity.[39] This creation of identity was vital in the face of industrialization and led to a

Instructions for this Rhineland-style castle came with the rare additional
outfit for the largest Anchor set, No. 34.

Images from an early Richter's Blocks box lid (top) contrasted with that from
a set made in East Germany.

romantic reverence for the past, and hence an interest in the conservation of historic buildings such as the castles on the Rhine. The wealth generated from industrialization made such ventures possible. With the appearance of Richter's Blocks in the 1880s the opportunity arose to reinforce many of these ideas in a way that was affordable, at least for the middle classes. The fact that the blocks were mass produced and exported was part of the success of German industrialization, but the world suggested in the instruction books and even in the colours and shapes of the bricks themselves was more ideal than realistic. Realism, in terms of designs for children to build that might be part of their everyday surroundings, only came much later, by which time the factory in Rudolstadt had been consumed by the East German 'miracle'.

Richter's blocks, like Wagner's stage settings, have just sufficient realism to be recognized as German. They are part of creating 'Germanity' or *Heimat* and its exportation to the rest of the world.

CHAPTER THREE

▨ Meccano
▨
and Making Visible
▨
▨ How Things Work

T IS HARD TO DENY THAT MECCANO, of all the construction toys, is about engineering rather than architecture, since the boxes it came in were labelled 'Engineering for Boys'. However, it claims its place here because it has inspired the work of two world-renowned modern British architects, Norman Foster and Richard Rogers, both of whom were boys who played with Meccano.

Meccano was first patented in 1901 by a clerk in Liverpool called Frank Hornby. He devised a system that he initially called 'Mechanics Made Easy: an adaptable mechanical toy'. This consisted of perforated steel strips, wheels and axles assembled with nuts and bolts that enabled his children to build mechanical models that could be taken to pieces and reassembled into something else. In this sense, Meccano was like a set of building blocks, and the parts had to be fixed together by the builder, but what was different about it was that it made structures and mechanisms rather than buildings. Hornby changed the name to Meccano in 1907.[1] If nothing else, Hornby's choice of name resulted in a lot of other construction toys with names ending in 'o', such as Bayko, Mobaco and Juneero, all of which feature in later chapters of this book. There were also a large number of very close copies of Meccano, some of which, such as the Australian Ezy-Bilt, even blatantly copied many of the Meccano models in their instruction manuals. However, for all collectors out there (with good eyesight or a magnifying glass) all genuine Meccano parts are stamped 'Meccano'.

Like Richter's Blocks, Meccano was a very successful product and was sold all over the world; outside Britain, there were factories in France, Germany, the United States and Argentina. Over the years of its production, which continues largely in France at the time of writing, the range of Meccano parts expanded from the basic generic perforated strips, angle girders, brackets, wheels and rods that came in the first sets to highly specialized parts like the Dredger Bucket (Part 131), of which you would need a great many to build a model dredger, or the Ship's Funnels (Part 138a) which came in a range of colours to represent the shipping line of your choice. The complete range of parts (or Parts, in Meccano parlance) was illustrated on the back of the instruction manuals, so that the young owner of one of the smaller sets could see, save up for, or wheedle an aunt into buying some of the more advanced items. The most expensive single part was the Geared Roller Bearing (Part 167), which was manufactured from 1928 to 1940 and cost £1.[2] A craftsman builder in southern England was earning around £3 or £4 a week at this time, depending on hours worked,[3] so this was a pretty costly Part.

As well as the expense that enthusiasts would have to incur, Meccano was not entirely truthful about what could be built with the sets. The Giant Blocksetting Crane on the cover of the Meccano Manuals could be made only if you had a vast collection of expensive parts, including the Geared Roller Bearing, which had been discontinued in 1940[4] long before the image was first being used for the cover of the 1948 Meccano Manuals.[5] Not even the huge Meccano Outfit No. 10 could come close to building this model. Similar flexibility with the truth can be seen on the box lid of the Aeroplane Constructor Outfits, which first appeared in 1931. Initially they used a picture of a biplane fighter, which was more or less what the Outfits could make. Later boxes showed a streamlined airliner that was nothing at all like the fairly clunky, albeit charming, aircraft that you can build with the parts supplied; these had not changed although the picture had.

The beauty of Meccano is that it allows the construction of working machines, from motorcars to dockyard cranes, from transporter bridges to lathes and drill presses. The parts include not only the strips, plates and girders to make the structure of the models but also gears, sprocket chains, pulleys and motors (clockwork, steam or electric) to activate them. One of Meccano's other

A Meccano box lid from around 1926, with tempting images of things that could not actually be built with the No. 3 Outfit.

INSTRUCTIONS for OUTFIT No. 9   COPYRIGHT BY MECCANO LIMITED   49.9
BINNS ROAD, LIVERPOOL 13, ENGLAND

The Giant Blocksetting Crane, which could not be built even with the biggest available
Meccano Outfit: parts such as the Geared Roller Bearing could no longer
be bought in 1949, when this instruction manual was produced.

satisfying features, apart from the all-metal solidity of the finished models (plastics played no part in Meccano until the 1960s) is that the things you can make from it are almost always a lot bigger than the box it comes in.

Was Meccano used for making model buildings? The instruction manuals occasionally included plans for making buildings, but these were very few and far between. A quick glance at the *Instructions for No. 1 Outfit* from 1946, a date when any keen British boy engineer might be expected to be interested in building, at the very least, a prefabricated steel bungalow to replace bomb-damaged brick houses,[6] reveals designs for forty different models. There are six different types of cranes, three different aeroplanes, seven machine tools, and several pieces of furniture. There is even an 'Eskimo boy and sledge' (you could build both), but no buildings. There is an occasional building in one or two of the Manuals for larger Outfits (Meccano always referred to things in capitals) but not many. The most splendid is the 1938 'Modern House', model 10.9 for the No. 10 Outfit.[7] This is a two-storey house in the Moderne Streamlined (late-Art-Deco) style, with wide windows and a flat roof terrace for sunbathing. This model was replaced quite rapidly by the 'Mobile Workshop'. Even when the Modern House was in the Manual, very few boys, or their parents, could have afforded the huge No. 10 Outfit. Most had to be content with ogling it in the pages of the Meccano catalogues, and very few were exposed to the idea of making Meccano buildings.

The Meccano Magazine, published from 1916 to 1981, did occasionally print ideas for making Meccano buildings, but the title of one such article – 'Off the Beaten Track'[8] – makes clear how unusual this was in the general Meccano scheme of things. Nonetheless, Meccano buildings did continue to feature in the magazine, with the last such article appearing in 1975[9] and showing models of two ecclesiastical London buildings: the church of St Martin-in-the-Fields and St Paul's Cathedral. The Meccano Magazine even held occasional architectural-model-building competitions. So there were Meccano buildings, but they were generally unusual, and probably considered something of a distraction from the more orthodox cranes, liners and locomotives, which never needed any explanation or apology. However, what is undeniable is that Meccano was very much about revealing how things worked and this can be directly linked to the ethos, if not perhaps the reality, of what has been called 'High-Tech' architecture.

Norman Foster (now Baron Foster of Thames Bank) and Richard Rogers, (now Baron Rogers of Riverside) have been two of the leading lights of British architecture in the last quarter of the twentieth century and beyond. Both are reported to have enjoyed playing with Meccano, and even to attribute their careers to this.[10] The Design Museum in London, in its biographies of notable designers, even mentions Rogers's Meccano set as an influence on the design of the Pompidou Centre in Paris.[11]

Foster's 2010 biography by Deyan Sudjic, director of the Design Museum, describes how as a boy growing up in a Manchester suburb in the 1940s, Foster's pocket money went on construction sets, notably Trix and Meccano, and he spent many hours exploring their capabilities. In an interesting link to the first chapter of this book (and to Trix), he also used to take the tram to the city centre to gaze at the model locomotives in the window of the Bassett-Lowke shop.[12] Foster's buildings, like those of Rogers, have been seen as originators of the style of architecture known as High-Tech, a description that first appeared in Joan Kron and Suzanne Slesin's 1978 book *High Tech: The Industrial Style and Source Book for The Home*.[13] According to architect and writer Colin Davies, the characteristics of High-Tech Architecture are industrial production, the use of technology and imagery from outside the building industry, flexibility, honesty and the use of steel and glass. Its key visual features are exposed structure and exposed services.[14] With the exception of the glass, these could all be found in Meccano (and glass is simply represented by the spaces in between the structural components). They are certainly also found in Foster's Hong Kong and Shanghai Bank in Hong Kong (1986).

Davies points out that the architects involved did not like the use of the description High-Tech, and the introduction to his 1988 book *High Tech Architecture* also suggested that the style was already at an end. This may have been an exaggeration, as what we might call the Meccano style is now used widely for modern transport buildings, particularly airports and railway stations.

It is likely that Meccano influenced a number of engineers and architects all over the world. It had a factory in France by the mid-1920s,[15] and Meccano was being promoted and sold there prior to this, with Meccano France registered as a company in 1912.[16] It is possible that the designer and architect–engineer Jean Prouvé could have played with the toy as a boy, although Meccano is not mentioned as an influence in his early life. He does, however, write of having a vocation to be a blacksmith (*forgeron*) from the age of ten, and of the processes of forging, shaping, adjusting and bolting steel becoming part of his thoughts and

The 1986 Hong Kong and Shanghai Bank, designed by Norman Foster,
looks as if it has been assembled from Meccano-like components.

actions as a child, whether to make a habitable house in the garden, or to construct a car with steering and brakes.[17] As a metalworker and designer with his own workshop (like the village blacksmith of old) Prouvé made building components of lightweight fabricated steel components, like Meccano, but he also wrote impassioned texts on the need for the industrialization of construction.[18] One of his early products was the first system of movable and demountable metal partitions for commercial buildings.[19] His designs often incorporated movable metal shutters for controlling light and ventilation, such as those he designed for the 1953 apartment building at 5 Square Mozart in Paris.[20] In this project the shutters not only slide up and down, but can also be tilted outwards, allowing light in but providing shade from direct sunlight; this makes them Prouvé's interpretation in steel of the traditional wooden shutters used on many buildings in France and the Mediterranean. While supremely practical, this system could also be seen as revealing the fascination for movement and change that Meccano construction makes visible.

The essence of Meccano, however, is that it is a kit of parts that can make a model of almost anything. This is very different from most modern construction toys, which tend to make one type of model. Even the smallest Meccano outfits provided plans for making a wide range of vehicles, machines, household objects, cranes and even dragons and dinosaurs in the inter-war years. The idea of Meccano was that it made 'a new toy every day'.[21] This slogan was used in Meccano advertising in the US from 1917 (when the featured model for boys to make was a tank) to 1926.[22] It is a sign of how Meccano kept abreast of contemporary developments in technology that they were advertising how to build a model tank almost as soon as the real thing appeared in action.

In the 1926 advert, there is the added slogan at the bottom 'As Easy as Building with Blocks'. However, when it comes to real buildings, 'a new toy every day' is not really what is needed, since buildings are generally more fixed than that. This kit-of-parts approach, which can make a new structure every day, means that Meccano is very different from the architecture that is sometimes described as being like Meccano. A good example is the Centre Pompidou in Paris, completed in 1977 and designed by Richard Rogers and Renzo Piano. This building was intended to be changeable, in plan, section and elevation, and was in fact described as 'a giant Meccano set'.[23] The reality is somewhat different, as Kron and Slesin point out: the Centre Pompidou, which looks as if it is made from a collection of standardized parts, is in fact all purpose-designed,[24] and the building is inevitably relatively permanent.

There are structures that are more like Meccano, such as Prouvé's 800 pre-fabricated houses, made in 1944. These were valuable and versatile because of the way they could be dismantled and rebuilt without any damage.[25] However, they are not entirely like Meccano; although they were made of metal and could be taken apart and reassembled, when the parts were put together they could only make the same thing as before – a small house.

Richard Rogers is quoted as again making the analogy with Meccano with reference to the Lloyds Building in London, completed in 1986.[26] In appearance this building is very Meccano-like, partly because of its silvery colour, similar to the nickel finish of the earliest Meccano sets, and partly because its structure and the way the building is organized and serviced is so clear. All the elements of the building are visibly differentiated from one another: the central atrium over the dealing floor, the stair towers and the toilet pods. The external cladding is largely metal, although the external columns are concrete. Finally, the services for dis-tribution of ventilation, heating and cooling are draped over the exterior of the building so as to leave the interior spaces clear, and the lifts run up the outside of the towers. Every part is separate from the rest and exposed to view. The whole thing looks like a working Meccano model, and you can watch the lifts moving up and down as if powered by the Meccano No. 1 Clockwork Motor. But again, the Meccano analogy is only skin deep, as the building is inevitably made of specialized components that were designed for that specific purpose. It is not an assembly of standardized parts, and the main structure is not metal, but reinforced concrete.

In many ways these Meccano-like buildings are less reflective of Meccano as such, but rather of the tradition of the engineering structures of the Industrial Revolution. These began in Britain with the Iron Bridge (1781)[27] at the epony-mous Ironbridge in Shropshire, and continued into the mid-nineteenth century with the Crystal Palace (1851) and the train sheds over the platforms of the great railway termini.

This tradition was notably displayed by Isambard Kingdom Brunel, appointed engineer for the Great Western Railway from London to Bristol in 1833, at the age of 27. At a directors' meeting in October 1835, where someone complained of the length of the line from London to Bristol, Brunel countered by suggesting building a steam ship so the line would go all the way to New

York.[28] He then worked with colleagues to design the steam ship Great Western (1838),[29] whose success allowed a traveller to buy a ticket to New York from Paddington Station. Since the first public railway only opened in 1825, this was a bit like offering a ticket to the Moon would have been in 1979.

Brunel's boldness of vision made him a celebrity in his age[30] and as the nineteenth century progressed, others contributed to the growing celebration of engineering in all its forms. The most notable structure of the time was the Crystal Palace of 1851, built to house the first World Expo, the Great Exhibition of the Works of Industry of all Nations.[31] This building certainly met all of Davies's criteria for High-Tech architecture. It was designed by Joseph Paxton, who began his career as gardener to the Duke of Devonshire and ended it as an adviser and director of the Midland Railway; he sketched it on a piece of blotting paper during a railway meeting. Nine days later the complete drawings were finished for a building that was to cover nineteen acres. The contractors gained access to the site on 30 July 1850 and the Great Exhibition opened on 1 May 1851; around 2,000 workers had completed the prefabricated iron and glass building, which was visited by over six million people before the Exhibition closed in October. The building was then taken down and re-erected, in an expanded form, in south London, where it stood until destroyed by fire on 30 November 1936. The title 'Crystal Palace' was given to Paxton's building by *Punch*, the humorous magazine, and lives on as the name of that part of London where it was re-erected.[32]

The buildings that superficially look like Meccano are not like it. They do not get taken apart and made into motor cars or railway engines whose origin, like that of Meccano, lies in engineering. The closest Meccano analogy is with the specialist Meccano Outfits that were introduced in the 1930s: the Aeroplane Constructor (1931) and the Motor Car Constructor (1932). Both of these contained a range of special parts that allowed the construction only of a range of aeroplanes or motor cars.[33] But, unlike the Constructor Outfits, Meccano-style buildings are usually made of hand-crafted components rather than mass-produced standard parts. However, they do indeed often have Meccano-like external moving and working parts, such as the lifts at Lloyds or the sun-scoops on the Hong Kong and Shanghai Bank.

It is perhaps fitting that the celebration of the architecture of Foster and Rogers in 1986 was combined with the work of another celebrated British architect, James Stirling, in an exhibition at the Royal Academy in London called

The 1997 Pompidou Centre in Paris, designed by Richard Rogers and Renzo Piano, appears to have been made from a Meccano-style kit-of-parts, although it is a one-off design.

The 1986 Lloyds Building was linked to Meccano by its architect Richard Rogers; however, the scaffolding just visible behind the ducts is perhaps more Meccano-like than the building.

simply 'Foster, Rogers, Stirling'.[34] Stirling's earlier buildings, such as the Engineering Building at Leicester University (with James Gowan, completed 1964) or the History Faculty Building for Cambridge University (with Michael Wilford, completed 1967), are very much celebrations of engineering. They are made of the same highly durable engineering bricks that were used to build the bridges and viaducts of the Industrial Revolution, and use the industrial glazing of factory roofs.

In the past engineers have not just waxed lyrical about the benefits of Meccano, they have used it to solve real problems by making mechanical analogue computing devices. For example, the Meccano Differential Analyser No. 2 is a programmable computer built in 1935 by J. B. Bratt at Cambridge University. It was used for calculations involved in designing the 'bouncing bombs' for the famous Dam Busters raid in the Second World War; it was then exported to New Zealand and used, with pleasing irony, to design the Benmore hydroelectric dam. Later it went on to calculate rabbit populations, the rabbit being a major introduced pest in New Zealand's grazing-based agriculture. The No. 2 is now on show at Auckland's Museum of Transport and Technology (MOTAT) as the only surviving differential analyser in the world.[35]

The Crystal Palace symbolized the era when 'With Steam and the Bible, the English traverse the globe'.[36] Meccano, although it did not appear until fifty years after the Crystal Palace, has been viewed by some as an integral part of Britain's past engineering excellence. Alec Issigonis, the ground-breaking designer of the Morris Minor and the Mini cars, was presented with a Number 10 Meccano Outfit when he retired from the motor industry in 1971,[37] and he founded the Issigonis Shield as an award for Meccano modellers, which is still presented today.[38] The eminent scientist Sir Harry Kroto has credited playing with Meccano for helping the research that won him the 1996 Nobel Prize for chemistry, and has lamented that Meccano's lessening popularity as a toy is linked to Britain's engineering decline.[39]

Certainly Meccano teaches an understanding of structures and mechanisms. While it may not be directly translated into buildings, celebrated architects, engineers and designers recall playing with it and acknowledge its influence on their work.

CHAPTER FOUR

Lott's Bricks and the Arts and Crafts Movement

OTT'S BRICKS AT FIRST LOOK AND FEEL LIKE RICHTER'S BLOCKS but they are British in a way that makes them the antithesis of their German counterpart. There are no medieval castles lurking in Lott's Bricks, just good plain British buildings, beautiful to look at because the proportions and materials are so right and the lines so simple. This reflects the ethos of the Arts and Crafts movement, which produced some of the best of British architecture. Significant examples range from artist and writer William Morris's home, the Red House, designed by Morris and the architect Philip Webb incorporating large expanses of plain brickwork, to Edward Prior's church of St Andrew's, Roker, with its concrete purlins and handmade wooden doors. Lott's Bricks allow you to play with these ideas at home.

Lott's Bricks were manufactured in Bushey, Hertfordshire, and are still celebrated in the local museum. Their date of origin is unclear: Lott's sets have a copyright of 1911 but first appeared at the 1917 British Industries Fair, where Queen Mary bought a set – without an instruction manual, as these were not yet printed. Still, royal endorsement and strong marketing after the armistice of 1918 produced a successful toy, which was much loved.[1] They are British in so many ways, and soon replaced Richter's Blocks in popularity, possibly because of the anti-German feelings at that time.[2] During the First World War, imports from Germany disappeared, and the gap was filled by increases in manufacture of existing British toys and the development of new local products.[3] Lott's Bricks were not only a replacement for Richter's Blocks but also the realization of the dream of their creator, Ernest Lott, for a simpler version that would make British buildings.[4] To do this he called on the services of the Arts and Crafts architect Arnold Mitchell to design the sets of bricks and the buildings that could be made from them.

Lott's Bricks not only feel similar to Richter's Blocks (they were made of similar materials), but the early sets also feature the same three colours of cream, red and blue. Alas, as many a child (or later collector) discovers, the blocks are not interchangeable: the German ones are based on a 2.5-centimetre module whereas Lott's are based on 1 inch (2.54 cm). Inevitably, because of their similar appearance blocks from both sources have been muddled over time, which can make for unstable buildings and bad language.

Early sets of Lott's Bricks show a very English village on the box lid with cottages and villas, a guildhall and a village hall, a war memorial and a church on the top of the hill. In the instructions the church is labelled 'Cathedral' but sits low in the manner of Arts and Crafts architect William Lethaby's modest Brockhampton Church in Herefordshire; this could just be because high structures in Lott's do tend to be unstable.

All buildings in the original Lott's village were made from just eleven different bricks, in various shapes half an inch (1.27 cm) and one inch (2.54 cm) thick, with a chimney block shaped to fit over the ridge of the folded printed cardboard roof. In contrast, the full Richter range extends to over 3,000 different types of brick. Another difference between Lott's and Richter's is that the former are all rectangles or triangles whereas Richter's blocks are far more complex, with many variations of arches and pinnacles.[5] Most surviving Lott's Bricks are red, blue and cream, as the black of the early sets soon disappeared. This limited range is much more like a British vernacular village, where every house is built of the same materials to almost the same design with small differences in detail.

To make the complete village would take a lot of Lott's Bricks, since the largest set was needed to build the Cathedral. However, a Boat House and a Market Cross could be made with the small sets. Like Richter's Blocks, adding a Set 1A to a Set 1, for example, gave the equivalent of a Set 2, although plans for different models were supplied with each converting set as well. This system encouraged children to ask for Lott's for Christmas and birthdays so as to build up the collection, although this was a slightly more expensive way of acquiring the numbers of blocks needed for the large models.

(Top) The Arts and Crafts village world of Lott's Bricks, as pictured on the box lid.

(Above) Brockhampton Church, designed in 1902 by the Arts and Crafts architect W. R. Lethaby; Nikolaus Pevsner described the building as sitting somewhere between historicism and modernism.

What could be built with the smallest set differs markedly from the gloomy gravestones and gateways of the German precursor. Lott's Set 0 came with instructions for six buildings: Cottage, Seaside Shelter, Cart-shed, Garage, Workshop and Summer House. The latter two even had flat roofs. This may be an early example of modernism; the first flat-roofed houses in Britain were Charles Quennell's concrete-block flat-roofed semi-detached cottages built for Crittalls in Braintree around 1918.[6] The roofs apart, however, these small houses are ordinary and more friendly than the gravestones of the small Richter sets.

The instructions that come with Lott's also make a very different world from that of the German toy. The Richter designs show each individual building in an isolated setting. The various buildings on the Lott's box lid are shown in a single, almost believable setting, with toy people (possibly Hornby O gauge figures). Given enough bricks and green felt, and an indulgent parent, the whole scene in Lott's could have been made. It was one that seems to have stepped from the pages of William Morris's *News from Nowhere*.

Morris's novel is a work of utopian socialism and a paean to Arts and Crafts ideals. During his hero's trip up the Thames, Morris refers to the replacement of cast-iron Gothic bridges – 'old enemies' – with 'handsome oak and stone'.[7] When it comes to the cathedral towards the end of the book Morris describes a church that is plain, with no decorations in the simple nave, chancel and transepts. The Lott's windows might not be of 'the graceful Oxfordshire fourteenth-century type' of Morris's description but their simplicity and regularity in the wall reproduces the essence if not the fact of the old.[8] The Mote-House in *News from Nowhere* with its steeply pitched roof and high wall could be describing Lott's Guildhall. It is hard to make a steeply pitched roof when the only roof available is a 45-degree pitch, but Mitchell's design compensates for the roof slope with a parapet at the eaves and a tall chimney to add height. In the novel there is also an arcade where the market was held.[9] This has its counterpart in the ground floor of Lott's Guildhall, or in the Market Hall from another Lott's set. Morris also notes that in the villages of *News from Nowhere*, the Church and Mote-House are the chief buildings, as are their equivalents on the Lott's Bricks box lid.[10] The little Boat House could be taken as the landing stage at Hammersmith described by Morris,[11] and the small, low, detached houses are typical of his rural utopia.[12] Only the Shrine or War Memorial does not appear in Morris's text, in which monuments have disappeared in favour of trees,[13] unless it is imagined as a Market Cross at the centre of the village marketplace.[14]

The Lott's lid shows an English village recreated in an Arts and Crafts image full of solid, plain buildings that sit together within a wider landscape. This is not an architects' fantasy of what an ideal place might be, such as that of the Welsh 'village' of Portmeirion which was entirely created by its designer and owner Clough Williams Ellis.[15] It is an ideal founded on reality, reflecting simple, honest social arrangements, and even the later sets of Lott's Bricks maintained the village imagery on the box lid.

Although he only worked on Lott's at the start, the delightful simplicity of the toy was the work of Arnold Mitchell. Mitchell is what might be described as a 'bread-and-butter' Arts and Crafts architect, rather than the roast dinner of Richard Norman Shaw (of the previous generation) or the delicately flavoured poached salmon of C. F. A. Voysey (a near contemporary). He is mentioned once in Margaret Richardson's book on Arts and Crafts architects as passing through the office of the firm Ernest George and Peto.[16] Mitchell's domestic architecture was publicized in the various volumes of *The Studio*, where he was said to be very proficient in the art of economical house planning based on making small houses feel both spacious and comfortable.[17] He was particularly fond of houses with a series of gables,[18] such as those he did in Hampstead Garden Suburb, north London, at Temple Fortune Lane (in 1908) and Meadway Close (in 1910).

It is no surprise, therefore, that gabled houses are a feature of the plans in the larger sets of Lott's Bricks (Sets 3, 4 and 5), which are supplied with additional valley-piece cardboard roofs to allow their construction. These pieces first appear in the converting Set 2A, which had plans for a Parish Hall with gabled porch and the Four-gabled House (see illustration overleaf). They were based on Mitchell's prize-winning entry for the first ever Ideal Home Exhibition in 1908; this was a design for an inexpensive cottage in the £500 class. The contemporary commentary in *The Builder* magazine liked the plan but was critical of the high roof, which contained two floors of accommodation, noting, 'high roofs may be thought picturesque but they are not practical, and this is not the way to design modern cottages; it is an anachronism.'[19] The Lott's version, of necessity, has only one storey in its four-gabled 45-degree pitched roof, thereby neatly responding to the criticism of *The Builder*.

Plans for a building with two gables on one side, not unlike the houses on Temple Fortune Lane, are shown in Lott's Tudor Blocks (also shown overleaf). This was a 1922 addition to the series, with black-and-cream patterned bricks and green-tiled roofs. However, in the early years of Arnold Mitchell, Lott's

SOME OTHER TUDOR, LOTT'S BRICKS, AND LODOMO MODELS.

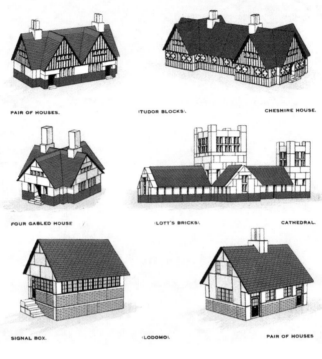

PAIR OF HOUSES. (TUDOR BLOCKS). CHESHIRE HOUSE.

FOUR GABLED HOUSE (LOTT'S BRICKS). CATHEDRAL.

SIGNAL BOX. (LODOMO). PAIR OF HOUSES

Arnold Mitchell's 34 and 36 Temple Fortune Lane, Hampstead Garden Suburb (above), can be compared with the instructions for making a two-gabled house (top, top left) in Lott's bricks; the four-gabled house (top, middle left) echoes Mitchell's prizewinning Ideal Home competition entry.

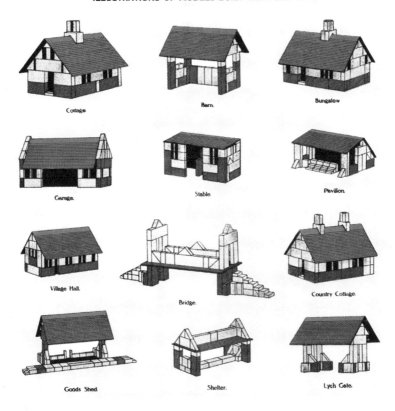

Cottage

Barn.

Bungalow

Garage.

Stable.

Pavilion.

Village Hall.

Bridge.

Country Cottage.

Goods Shed.

Shelter.

Lych Gate.

Examples from the instruction booklet for Lott's cottages (top) are comparable with Randall Wells' prizewinning cottage at Letchworth Garden City.

retained its simplicity in what could be made with the limited block modules, and one of the most frequently occurring buildings is the simple gabled cottage or small house.

For Mitchell, as for many architects of his generation, the cheap cottage, built in a stripped Arts and Crafts manner and sparely furnished to give dignity to the lives of its inhabitants, had become a holy grail. The cheap cottage was, perhaps, the epitome of Arts and Crafts architecture, since of necessity it had to be simple and undecorated. It echoed the German architect Hermann Muthesius's description of the larger buildings of architects like Charles Voysey as being '...of the simplest, so that there is always an air of primitiveness about his houses';[20] and as G. A. T. Middleton observed in 1906, 'In no class of dwellings are the conditions so simple as in workmen's cottages, yet the opportunities for variation are endless...'.[21] No surprise, therefore, that the limited palette of Lott's Bricks could easily be turned to the building of simple cottages, varying only in terms of window and door placements and in what they were called in the instructions (Bungalow, House or Cottage).

The editor of *The Spectator* at that time, John Strachey, believed that one route to the cheap cottage was through improved forms of construction, provided these were fit for their purpose.[22] He instigated a competition for cottages to cost no more than £150 and secured some land in the new garden city of Letchworth for building, exhibiting and selling the entries. The cost was calculated as the maximum a landowner could afford to spend on building given that the rural labourer could only afford £8 a year in rent. The exhibition of 119 cottages was held in 1905.[23] Two of the winning designs follow the simple forms achievable in Lott's: the best detached cottage for no more than £35 per room by Randall Wells and the best wooden cottage by F. W. Troup[24] (now much altered).

Mitchell built his own ideal cottage at a cost of £110, looking exactly like one of the designs for Lott's.[25] A pair of cottages were first publicized in *The Times*,[26] but Mitchell went on to build a detached version of the same plan in the grounds of his own house, where for a time it masqueraded as an aviary to avoid the interference of the local council. Looking just like the Lott's Bungalow from Set 1, it had two bedrooms in the roof space; a living room with range, a parlour or third bedroom, a wash house, fuel store and larder below; and an earth closet accessed from outside. Sensibly, the chimney stack is in the centre of the plan. This was the usual position for Lott's cottages as the small sets only came with two half-inch (1.27-cm) chimney blocks, which really needed to be used together to make a realistic stack.

Small cottages could be made even more realistic using the Lott's Garden sets. These contained trees, shrubs, extra roofs, shells, sand and white cardboard picket fences; subsequently, trees and shrubs were included in the standard sets as well as fences (later made of green plastic). The fences were very good for linking small Lott's buildings together to make miniature farmyards peopled, at that time, with lead animals and farm workers. Playing with Lott's thus reinforced the British rural idyll. (An idyll that was promoted when the term 'cottage' was applied to many British housing estates built in the interwar period,[27] as if to suggest that life within the walls of such a building would have the slow pace and self-reliance of those in a novel by George Eliot or Thomas Hardy.) This idyll was also the backdrop for *News from Nowhere* and permeated much of the Arts and Crafts movement through various attempts to establish rurally based artistic communities, such as designer C. R. Ashbee's Guild of Handicrafts in the Cotswolds.[28]

Although Lott's could be seen as reinforcing the Arts and Crafts ideal, it provided plans for other buildings. The seaside is featured in plans for Seaside Shelters, a Pierrot Stage, and a Beach Café; there was also a Factory and a flat-roofed Bonded Warehouse. The Factory, with its projecting capping stones above the flat roof, recalls Voysey's factory for Sandersons, although the proportions are different. Garages appeared, showing how the world was changing.

Mitchell was known as a designer of schools. Two of his are in the form of the large gabled, brick country house – Orley Farm School, Harrow (1901) and St. Felix School, Southwold (1902). Of more relevance to the Lott's version is University College School in Hampstead (1907), again built in red brick, and set out as three related blocks, the central block being emphasized by its high pitched roof. This monumental approach to school design partly arose from the German tradition of grouping classrooms around a large central hall[29] but also relates to the medieval college tradition of Oxford and Cambridge, where the central entrance gate building is higher than the rooms grouped around the quadrangle within; this is seen in the Lott's College Building overleaf. There were not enough bricks in the larger Lott's sets to make a full quadrangle, but the effect is similar. The accompanying School Chapel is one of two designs (the other, more modernist in feel, featured in Set 3A [see page 61]), along with the flat-roofed School – still heated, it appears, by burning coal. Although based on

ILLUSTRATIONS OF MODELS BUILT WITH BOX 4.

College Building.

School Chapel.

Sanatorium.

Beacon Tower

Guildhall.

Warehouse.

47

(Above and opposite) Suggestions for making schools and chapels in Lott's Bricks; schematic plan and section layouts are given elsewhere in the instruction booklet.

Bridge, Box 3A.

School Chapel, Box 3A.

Terminus Station, Box 3A.

Warehouse,
Box 4A.

Railway Station, Box 3A.

Market Cross,
Box 3A.

Italian Tower.
Box 4A.

Workshop, Box 4A.

School, Box 4A.

58

Arts and Crafts models, some of these buildings foreshadow a much more modern style, owing to the minimal detail possible with the limited range of blocks.

Lott's Tudor bricks have already been mentioned. They included new pieces to make the black-and-white framing, and larger sets had more elaborately patterned bricks for a full-blown Elizabethan Tudor façade. These additional bricks moved Lott's away from the superb simplicity of the original. A further change came with the introduction, in 1929, of Lodomo (see page 56) with its doors, windows and brick patterning.[30] This change still only produced 14 different elements in the small sets. The instruction books were also changed to show how the printed bricks were used. Some earlier designs were updated, such as the Pierrot Stage which now had a brick-patterned plinth, but new designs like the flat-roofed Seaside Bungalow and the Aeroplane Hangar appeared. One more change occurred in the building sets[31] with the late introduction of Wonderbrix for small children. The same material was used to make patterned bricks in the form of whole gable ends, and wall pieces with the doors and windows moulded into them, still roofed with printed, hinged cardboard.

The wonder of Lott's Bricks is the very small palette of blocks and the wide variety of buildings that can be made with them, especially when compared with Richter's blocks. In this way Lott's Bricks again reflects the Arts and Crafts movement with its palette of few materials (brick, wood and stone), hand-made elements (limiting what could be achieved to a human scale and the skill of the craftsman), a general reflection of the British vernacular (use of gables, large chimney stacks, windows or bay windows in the plane of the wall), and accretion of simple rectangular forms.

The interior of the Arts and Crafts house was spare, its un-upholstered furniture with stick legs and gate-leg tables occupying minimal space, allowing the light from the windows to flood over the whole floor. The simplicity united with the plain architectural elements to make a visual whole. This was recognized by Arts and Crafts architects, with Raymond Unwin describing his Hampstead Garden Suburb houses as 'Plain Jane' and 'Mary Anne'.[32] There are intimations of this British love for the relatively simple and reduced in the difference between British and French Gothic Cathedrals; Puritanism and its ideal of a commonwealth may also have been an influence. A commonwealth suggests that if aspirations are limited and living is simple then everyone can have enough. In fact Morris first published *News from Nowhere* as a serial in the magazine *The Commonweal*, the socialist journal of which he was the editor from 1885 to 1890.[33] Simple living that involved use of head and hands and everyone having enough but not too much was as much the aim of Morris's socialism as of his attitude to architecture. This is reflected in the smaller buildings of the Arts and Crafts movement.

The elements of Arts and Crafts architecture are limited, and it is this minimalism that made architectural historian Nikolaus Pevsner see this movement as a precursor to modernism. He describes how Muthesius came back from his survey of English houses with a belief in 'reason and simplicity in building and art.'[34] The subtitle of Pevsner's *Pioneers of Modern Design* is: *From William Morris to Walter Gropius*. But the movement towards modernism might also be a journey that started from a rejection of Richter's Blocks – castles, crenellations, German Gothic – in favour of the plain cottages and British simplicity of Lott's Bricks.

Simplicity, however was not modernism. For Morris and his followers the socialist ideal meant that life had to be simple so that all could have a dignified life. However, Pevsner argues that modernism in the time of Gropius reflected an industrial ideal, with society based on the fruits of science and technology and high-speed travel, even if this meant less personal security and times of 'hard struggles'.[35] Simplicity is used here to represent the most building for the least cost, since industrialism is essentially about profit. This capitalist motive was recognized by Morris in *News from Nowhere* when he described the castles on the Rhine as being made for the same purpose as the railways – for extracting taxes from people. For Morris the railways had stopped people sending goods by water, forcing them to use the new means of transport at greater cost.[36]

As shown earlier, there is a link between the success of Richter's blocks and German industrial might. Lott's Bricks may reflect a different view of industrialism. The success of the toy was said to be guaranteed when Queen Mary bought that first box, but they never had the international sales Richter achieved. Through Arnold Mitchell's involvement with the design of the bricks and the buildings at the start, Lott's were linked with the Arts and Crafts movement and its inherent socialist-based simplicity. This same simplicity means you can build modernist buildings as well as cottages and cart sheds. However, as we will see in Chapter 12, in the discussion of Arkitex, there comes a point in the reductionism of late modern architecture where it is virtually impossible to make anything other than the prescribed building with the limited kit of parts available. The beauty of Lott's Bricks is that they could make very realistic modern buildings, as in the flat-roofed School, but they were also capable of making so very much more.

CHAPTER FIVE

Wenebrik and the (Un-modern) Steel House

W ENEBRIK IS RARE IN BEING A METAL CONSTRUCTION set that makes metal buildings. The rarity is paralleled in architecture: despite the best efforts of some architects, such as Jean Prouvé in France and Buckminster Fuller in the US (of whom more later) the all-metal building is also not a common sight.

However, sometimes a metal heart beats beneath a different skin, as in the steel-frame house. Here the metal frame is seen as liberating the building, enabling it to be built easily on sloping sites and enforcing a rational approach through the frame module and structure – whether or not this is clad in metal. The architect and historian Neil Jackson ties the emergence of the modern steel house to two 1929 designs (Richard Neutra's *Lovell Health House* in Los Angeles and Pierre Chareau's *Maison de Verre* in Paris) because both houses had a steel frame.[1] There is, however, an earlier history of almost all-metal houses going back to the late eighteenth century in Britain, with a cast-iron prefabricated lock-keeper's cottage at Tipton Green in Staffordshire.[2] This was essentially a cottage made of metal, with flanged cast-iron wall panels (not a metal frame as a generator of architecture). From this evolved another history of prefabricated cottage-style buildings with corrugated-iron walls and roofs, which were exported to places including Australia and California to house settlers and gold miners.

5

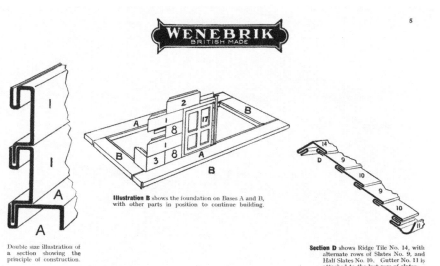

Illustration B shows the foundation on Bases A and B, with other parts in position to continue building.

Double size illustration of a section showing the principle of construction.

Section D shows Ridge Tile No. 14, with alternate rows of Slates No. 9, and Half Slates No. 10. Gutter No. 11 is attached to the last row of slates.

A Wenebrik box lid (top) and a page from the instruction manual showing how the folded metal wall and roof parts interlock.

Wenebrik sets, too, make cottage-style metal buildings; not as frame with cladding but as metal bricks and tiles slotted together. These interlocking parts are made of tinplate – very thin steel plated with tin – and coloured using offset chromolithography, a process used for toys from the late nineteenth century.[3] Normally, printed tinplate was assembled using tabs and slots to make toy cars or boats and most early tinplate toys were made in Germany, by companies such as Bing. Because tinplate was light it was less costly to export, so firms switched from the traditional material, wood, to the new. Wenebrik is unusual in being a British tinplate construction toy.[4]

Wenebrik sets were made in Birmingham by William Bailey, appearing in 1916 and continuing until the 1930s.[5] The same manufacturers made another metal set, Kliptiko, which consisted of a series of rolled ⅜-inch (9.5 mm) diameter metal tubes, straight and curved, that could be slotted together at their ends. Plates, pulleys and wheels were also available so that a whole series of models were possible, said a 1930s advertisement: '…bridges, towers, factory machinery, elevators, conveyors, cranes, ships, trams, buses, cars, in fact everything a town contains!'[6] Boys are shown exclusively on the box lids of Kilptiko but the same advertisement quoted above stated that Wenebrik was for girls, who could use it to make the buildings for the town. Girls are shown on the Wenebrik box lids, although they are outnumbered by boys. Both sets had disappeared by the start of the Second World War.[7]

To construct a Wenebrik building, the first pieces are set in a metal base plate ring, also slotted together from shiny hollow rectangular metal sections. The pieces stack up using a fold and tab system, which is as fiddly as it sounds, although maybe less so than Meccano.[8] In some ways making it is more like making a real house since, for example, the roof is made from tiny metal tiles, though rather than working from the eaves up, the roof as a whole is prefabricated from the ridge down and then placed on the walls. At least the walls are built from the ground up. The realism of Wenebrik extends to having metal barge boards, gutters, doors and windows. Right-angle pieces made the corners, and hexagonal pieces were also provided with the larger sets for making towers. The tinplate pieces were also coloured: a realistic if bright red for the wall 'bricks' and chimney stacks, and green for the unglazed door and window frames, roof tiles, gutters, and barge boards. These colours closely matched the early red and green Meccano sets, although those did not appear until 1926, 10 years after the launch of Wenebrik.[9]

What you can make with Wenebrik is constrained by the technology and small number of components. Every building is based on a pitched-roof gable-ended house. The model Factory made with the largest set (no. 5) is just such a house; it has three storeys and windows regularly spaced across the façade, but with an attached factory chimney to one side. It somewhat resembles mills such as Richard Arkwright's Masson Mill of 1783, a large brick hipped-roof structure with a chimney at one end. These mills were powered by steam engines and so an exhaust chimney was required. Although the history of cast iron has been linked to the need to replace brick to make fireproof mills and factories,[10] in the Wenebrik factory the metal is being made to imitate brick.

The Wenebrik church is more realistic, since iron churches were made in the nineteenth century for export, as temporary churches in army camps, and for the expanding urban populations in Britain.[11] However, like the factory, the Wenebrik church looks as if made of masonry rather than being a true 'tin taber-nacle.'[12] The same is true of the houses and cottages; they look like typical British brick houses with pitched roofs. The only building models to stray from this are castles and forts; the interlocking of the wall pieces means that missing out every other one produces a fine imitation battlement. The scale of the wall pieces also gives the impression of solid stone, unlike the true metal house.

Metal houses had a history long before they were promoted by Le Corbusier's injunction in 1927 to create houses using industrial mass production in the way cars were produced.[13] The lock-keeper's cottage, mentioned above and now long demolished, is often cited as the earliest prefabricated building in Britain.[14] This single-storey house had walls of flanged storey-height cast-iron panels bolted together and interspersed with full-height metal windows. The interior was fin-ished with lath and plaster.[15] The makers of the cast-ironwork for the cottage probably drew on local experience of making sectional cast-iron bridges and iron ships. Near the cottage was the Horsley Iron Works which made canal bridges of iron and were the first manufacturers of a sectional iron steam ship, the *Aaron Manby* built in 1822, which was cast at Tipton and then shipped for assembly at Rotherhithe in London.[16] Several large prefabricated houses used this ship-building approach, and two are still used in Australia: one a private house in Melbourne,[17] the other, Corio Villa, in Geelong. The latter has been described as the most ornate prefabricated house in Australia and probably the world.[18] The story is that in 1855 the flat-packed house parts were abandoned on a wharf because the man who ordered them had died. They were discovered and

30

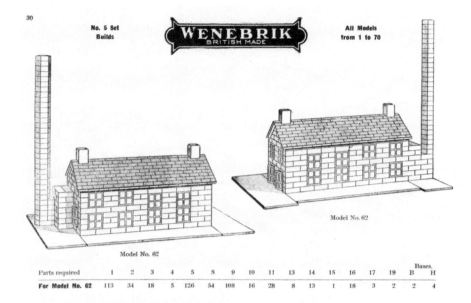

Parts required	1	2	3	4	5	8	9	10	11	13	14	15	16	17	19	Bases. B	H
For Model No. 62	113	34	18	5	126	54	108	16	28	8	13	1	18	3	2	2	4

The Wenebrik factory (top) compared with Arkwright's 1783 Masson Mill, Matlock Bath.

No. 3 Set
Builds

Model No. 41

Model No. 41

The Wenebrik Cottage that could be made with the No. 3 set (left) looks as if it might be built of stone; here it is contrasted with a true metal cottage, the Portable Iron Cottage, South Melbourne.

bought by a passer-by, Mr Alfred Douglas, a notable local citizen who held the first-ever public wool sale in Geelong[19] and was a founder-member of the Geelong branch of the Acclimatisation Society, responsible for importing exotic flora and fauna for settlement in Australia.[20] Douglas put up Corio Villa on its present site in 1856 without instructions, as the works where it was made had been destroyed by fire. The walls of Corio Villa were made by bolting together iron plates, and were later lined with wood. A truly beautiful house, it is fitting that lines written in 1885 on the death of its first owner included the phrase 'His life was just; he did not let the God-given talent rust.'[21]

However, solid metal houses, the nearest to a full size version of the Wenebrik system, are the rarefied end of the all-metal house. The real boom in prefabricated portable iron buildings came with the introduction of sheets of corrugated galvanized iron – which was strong, corrosion resistant and light, so easily transported – to clad the iron frame and roof trusses.[22] Even doors and shutters could be framed and clad with the material. The all-metal house could be prefabricated in modular parts, just like Wenebrik models, and then shipped for reassembly elsewhere. In the middle and latter parts of the nineteenth century, portable iron buildings became a staple for the colonies, not least because the cost of shipping them was so low: an iron house made useful ballast in a ship being sent out to come back laden with produce for the home country.[23]

Other early exports were prefabricated iron buildings for military campaigns and keeping the peace in unruly colonies. Charles D. Young and Co. made barracks and other buildings for camps in the UK at Aldershot and Colchester, so it was a simple step to advertise these internationally. Another firm, John Walker, had advertised similar products in *The Builder* in 1855.[24] Sadly, none of these military buildings had the style of a Wenebrik castle or fort. They were corrugated iron sheds of various sizes, looking most like an extruded portable cottage, with fitted loopholes through which soldiers could fire on unruly natives, unreasonably rebellious over the appropriation of their land.[25]

Although early structures exported to the colonies were of wood, such as the Manning Portable Colonial Cottage of around 1830,[26] metal had advantages apart from shipping weight. It is dimensionally stable and it can also be joined (by bolting) in a way that makes it easy to assemble and then take apart without damaging the material. The all-metal building, including metal frames to doors and windows, could be made by one manufacturer. It could be put up quickly with relatively unskilled labour, even if refinements like an inner lining of boards or plaster had to be done later. It was these pragmatic reasons that led to the importation of iron cottages to the new colonies. As historian Andrew Hassam commented,[27] these buildings were as light and portable as tents but more durable, if just as easily blown down during the course of putting them up.[28]

In 1853 over 6000 iron houses were imported into the state of Victoria, although the number of wooden houses imported in the same year was more than double this at nearly 16,000.[29] This suggests that even in the prefabrication of houses wood has been more important than metal, just as there are far more wooden building sets than metal, Wenebrik being a rare example. However, many early settlers must have quietly roasted under a hot tin roof in the unrelenting Australian summer in a house like the portable iron cottage in South Melbourne. This structure from 1853 has a wrought-iron frame of angles and T-sections and is clad in wide-pitch (5-inch/13-cm) corrugated iron for both walls and roof. Internally it is lined with boards, and boards also form the partition walls dividing up the simple space into six rooms. In form it is not unlike the Wenebrik cottage.

In the twentieth century, architects including Le Corbusier saw parallels between the industrial process for making cars and the application of this approach to houses. Only through mass production, it was argued, could housing be produced in sufficient quantities of sufficient quality.[30] Another argument for metal houses given by architects (and others) was the shortage of conventional materials following large-scale warfare.[31] This issue arose after both world wars.

In 1927, architect, designer and futurist Buckminster Fuller invented his first Dymaxion House.[32] The house was to be mass produced and deliver scientific (rationally planned, research-based) housing to all, by air rather than ship, thus bringing the science and technology of war to focus on the provision of housing.[33] This made it an updated version of the biblical polemic to turn swords into ploughshares.[34] The original hexagonal Dymaxion House, which never progressed beyond the prototype first exhibited in 1929, was hung from a central mast and was intended to be a revolution in terms of housing design.[35] The materials of this model were lightweight steel, duralumin (an aluminium alloy used in the aircraft industry in the 1930s) and plastics. The house was planned to be rented rather than owned, so even its tenure was in some way 'light weight'.[36] Its form echoes an earlier American prototype, the octagonal houses of Orson Fowler, publicized in his 1848 book *A Home for All*, although Fowler was an advocate for building in concrete rather than metal.[37] What both Fowler and

The mid-nineteenth-century Corio Villa, Geelong, an ornate metal house made from bolted cast-iron plates.

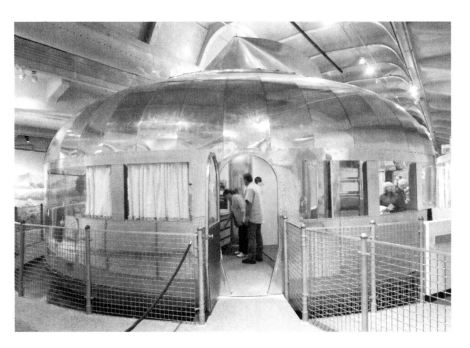

The exterior and interior of Buckminster Fuller's restored Dymaxion House, in essence little more than a metal tent, at the Henry Ford Museum in Detroit.

Fuller were searching for was maximum internal space for the minimum material enclosure, which would ideally be found by having spherical houses. Incidentally, both designers made much of how their houses came with fitted cupboards,[38] an essential feature if human living, with all its rather rectangular accoutrements, is fitted into polygonal forms; the cupboards neatly filled up left-over spaces.

Fuller's original Dymaxion house was never put into production and neither was his later circular aluminium version, often known as the Wichita House, first built after the Second World War by the Beechcraft aircraft company.[39] Like the first Dymaxion house, the walls remained non-load bearing; it was lightweight and forecast to be cheap once put into production. Sadly this never happened. The prototype Wichita House was bought for a dollar,[40] moved, and over the years extended and changed. It has now been restored to its original condition and is on show in the Henry Ford Museum in Detroit.

The irony in this is that another all-metal home, the Lustron House, did go into production as part of meeting the postwar housing shortage in the US. However, the steel-framed Lustron House, with its baked-enamel steel cladding in a range of cheerful colours, is a direct descendent of the colonial portable cottage and the type of simple metal cottage that could be made with Wenebrik. Just over 2,500 of these houses were produced over two years in the US – maybe not enough to be industrialized housing, but those that remain are still much loved.[41]

In Britain, the ordinary steel house emerged not because of an architectural dream of how metal might change the way houses were produced, but because of a shortage of conventional building materials after the First World War. Metal houses were made and lived in that might well have formed prototypes for the Wenebrik enthusiast. Adshead, Ramsey and Abercrombie – names associated with architecture, planning and architectural education in the UK[42] – were the architects for the 1919 Neo-Georgian steel-framed Dorlonco houses, which were erected by the steel firm of Dorman, Long at Dormanstown to house their workers. The war had increased steel production and a use for this capacity had to be found afterwards. Dorman, Long diversified by providing the steel for the Tyne and Sydney harbour bridges and patenting a steel-frame house, some 10,000 of which were built in the UK.[43] However, the bridges were better for profits, since the Sydney Harbour Bridge alone used 52,800 tonnes of steel[44] whereas all the houses might have accounted for 15,000 tonnes.[45] The Dorlonco steel-frame house was made in the factory and could be assembled on site by unskilled workers. The outside wall could be finished in metal lath and plaster, or even brick, and the inside was lined with plastered concrete blocks. These perfectly ordinary-looking houses had a useful life of 80 years before demolition in 1979.

In the 1920s there was a surplus capacity for steel-making, together with a lack of skilled builders to make the conventional houses that were needed. This led to the construction of steel-clad houses under the auspices of the nobility, in the persons of Lord Weir and the Duke of Atholl. Despite their good intentions the Weir house promptly ran into trouble from the trade unions for taking work away from skilled workers.[46] The Weir house was, in fact, a number of designs, with bungalows of timber frame clad in ⅛-inch (3 mm) steel sheet.[47] Later two-storey houses with both pitched and flat roofs were made on the same principle. The flat roof was made of steel sheet, like the wall cladding, and finished with felt.[48] The Atholl houses had a steel frame and walls clad externally with steel sheets and lined internally with fibreboard, and a conventional timber-truss tiled roof.[49] In appearance – apart from the flat-roofed Weir houses and bungalows which do look different – these are typical British interwar cottages that just happened to be made mostly of metal. Like any metal house (or car), and like Wenebrik itself, the steel rusted and had to be repainted.

Architects who liken the production of houses to the production of cars tend to gloss over this point. Cars are expected to have a relatively short life compared to houses (ten as opposed to fifty or more years). They also have multiple coats of factory-applied oven-baked paint. No-one has yet built an oven large enough to take a complete house. As the Ministry of Works commented in its 1944 investigation into alternative forms of house construction, 'Steel sheets contribute little to the functions of a wall except to the exclusion of rain....'[50] So, despite some 2,500 steel houses appearing in Scotland between the wars, none of these was an all-metal system of house construction like the Wenebrik toy, or even like the early portable metal cottages sent out to the colonies.

The British equivalent of the 'Dymaxion' in terms of unrealized potential was the all-steel prefabricated two-bedroom Portal Bungalow, named after the then Minister of Works. A single-storey prototype was exhibited in 1944 behind the Tate Gallery in London,[51] and it was intended as part of a programme to solve two problems. The first was the need to provide housing after the war for those returning and wishing to marry and start a family. Neatly, the second was to provide employment for these same returning soldiers in the steel and aluminium industries which had expanded to provide the tools of war and needed to find peacetime products to absorb this extra industrial capacity.

Although architect designed,[52] it was yet another prefabricated steel rectangular hut (or Wenebrik house Model 41). It was made in a car factory but, like many another prefabricated architect-designed house, it was put together by hand rather than on the production line and only one was ever made. Other part-metal prefabricated bungalows were eventually produced as part of this programme, such as the steel-frame asbestos-clad Arcon and the aluminium AIROH, which arrived on site in four prefabricated sections.[53]

Why is Wenebrik rare in being an architectural construction toy made of metal? And why are metal houses so uncommon? While there are modern houses that use steel frames and that are clad in colour-coated corrugated steel sheets where the finish is baked on in the factory, nowhere do these form the majority of the housing stock. In Australia, the site of all those early imported iron houses, steel framing reached an estimated 12% market share of new housing in 2005, and this framing would have been concealed by a variety of cladding.[54] Even the early portable iron houses would have been rarities. Contemporary descriptions and photos of gold-mining settlements show mainly tents and bark huts.[55]

Wenebrik itself provides some answers. The problem with the toy is that it becomes increasingly difficult to use, as the pieces get bent in the process of making models and taking them apart. The shape of the pieces means that you can't use the tried and tested rolling-pin method for flattening metal plates. Thin sheets of steel, such as corrugated cladding, suffer from the same kind of problem as, over time, dents appear. Like a car, an old, dented, steel-clad house looks rather unprepossessing. Other materials such as brick and even wood just age more gracefully. The other problem is one outlined above: steel rusts, as does Wenebrik, when exposed to air and water. Rusting inevitably happens to a house, unless preserved in a museum. This means that the house constantly, time-consumingly and expensively needs repainting to look good. That a construction material deteriorates in this way does not matter when it is used for a shed or even a factory, but houses (and toys) need to be made of sterner stuff. Family homes need to remain appealing and last a long time.

The all-steel house made like a car in a factory is still an attractive idea to designers who see this approach as a way of generating new and radical forms. The history of the steel house is somewhat different. Where they have been built in numbers they tend, like Wenebrik models, to look like conventional houses made of other materials – and perhaps it is because that is the way their users like them.

CHAPTER SIX

Lincoln Logs
and the
Log Cabin

L INCOLN LOGS ARE AS AMERICAN AS APPLE PIE (or, in a more Wild West reading of US history, as American as the country's four main food groups: 'beans, bacon, whiskey and lard'[1]). Lincoln Logs are miniature wooden logs with notched ends, which can be used to make log cabins like those that appear in Hollywood Westerns, as a backdrop to 'cowboys and Indians' in miniature. This toy has never gone out of production, perhaps because of the enduring quality of the games children play with it, and reproduction original sets are now available.[2] Log cabins may seem far from 'real' architecture, though their history as a building type is both long and honourable. In addition, Lincoln Logs have a real architectural connection because they were designed by an architect with a very famous name.

John Lloyd Wright was the son of architect Frank Lloyd Wright; he filed his first patent for Lincoln Logs in 1916, although the Vermont Novelty Company had also produced a building-block toy called 'Lincoln's Logs' in the first half of the nineteenth century.[3] John Wright's Lincoln Logs may have taken inspiration from his work in Japan on his Father's Imperial Hotel, with its cantilevered beams that interlocked where they met the corresponding beam cantilevering out from the next support. The principle was one of the measures Wright employed in an attempt to make a building that would withstand earthquakes.[4] Wright discussed the need to make a flexible structure and '...manage the joints in the design.[5] John, however, does not mention interlocking joints in his discussion of working on the Imperial Hotel, referring only to the fact his father had invented an earthquake-proof foundation.[6]

What is clear is that father and son working together was not a success. After being fired by his father, John Wright returned home from Japan and earned a living making wooden toys; one of these, which was a success, was Lincoln Logs.[7] Perhaps the appeal of the toy lies in the fact that its namesake and the most American of Americans, Abraham Lincoln, was born in a one-room log cabin in Kentucky[8] and what Lincoln Logs make best is a simple one-room log cabin. The log-cabin legend was further perpetuated by President Garfield, also born in one, whose career trajectory is described in his book *From Log-cabin to White House*.[9] Fiction may also have played a part: one Lincoln Logs model was called after Harriet Beecher Stowe's *Uncle Tom's Cabin* and brings to mind the description of the contented and charming (though now considered politically suspect) life in 'the small log building', one corner of which was the drawing room, and another the bedroom.[10]

Wright's toy made miniature log cabins from interlocking wooden 'logs', leaving gaps for doors and windows, and used thin wooden slats that sat on shaped gable end pieces to roof the building. The ends of the cylindrical Lincoln Logs have flat notches cut into them so they stack. In his patent application, Wright was to note that the interlocking components would give a stable structure that was also realistic, since American pioneers had made the walls of full size log cabins from stacked, notched logs.[11] The doorway is made by using logs shorter than the rest of the wall to leave a space, with alternating very short notched logs laid crossways at the side of the opening for support. A half log (cut lengthways) is used to provide a stable base. The gable is built up from a series of graded notched logs and the roof is two thin sheets of wood joined with a fabric hinge, like the hinged cardboard roofs of Lott's Bricks. A special chimney-piece could be positioned on the ridge. The materials thus make very stable small rectangular huts with limited openings, the ideal log cabin structure for a cold forest climate.

However, the sets, some coming with wheels, make other items too, such as the extremely unlikely Greyhound bus. The Greyhound Line had been consolidated in 1926[12] but it takes imagination to see much resemblance between the pile of logs with a wheel at each corner – even with the accessory bus driver figure – and the Greyhound buses of that period, such as the 1929 Will.[13]

No. 207. UNCLE TOM'S CABIN
REAR VIEW SAME AS No. 201 EXCEPT ONE LOG LOWER

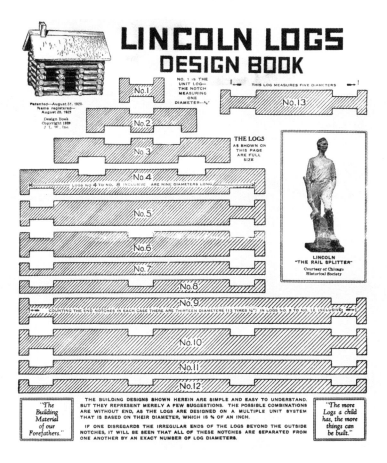

The numbered pieces from the 1929 Lincoln Logs instruction book (above), and a view of 'Uncle Tom's Cabin' (top) with the numbered pieces in place.

NO. 825.   GREYHOUND BUS

(Top) The Greyhound Bus that could be made from Lincoln Logs; the result is perhaps more appropriate for commuting Flintstones.

(Above) The box lid of a set of Lincoln Logs from the 1930s, reflecting the world of the pioneer in the American West.

Furniture was another idea, though small-scale pieces could only be made if the parts were held together with rubber bands. Permanent gluing was also suggested for making father a waste-paper basket or an outdoor hanging basket as a 'Gift suggestion for Grandmother', which rather defeated the object of being a 'toy'. These odd forays into the outer reaches of the imagination were not, unsurprisingly, as successful as the cabin, the fort, the general store and the bunk house that Lincoln Logs did so well.

The American log cabin probably came with early settlers from Europe, especially the Scandinavians and Germans.[14] The European tradition of building houses with walls made of horizontal notched logs spreads from Norway south through Germany to Switzerland and the Balkans and into Russia.[15] Moreover, the horizontal log tradition is rich, with many different methods of treating the overlapping logs at the corners and forming openings within the horizontal log walls, all demonstrating the skill of past craftsmen with the axe, adze and spokeshave. Even the forms of the buildings differ, from the simple rectangular cabin, which was sometimes subdivided internally, to the two-storeyed curved ceiling granaries of Silesia and the multi-storey, many-roomed Swiss farmhouse.[16]

Log houses are also part of Chinese tradition. In the northwest and southwest parts of China where there are still forests, walls are made of stacked logs and these are then plastered with mud and the roofs covered with grass sod,[17] very much in the tradition of Scandinavian log houses. Like Lincoln Logs these are notched on both sides so the stacked logs fit closely together and overlap at the corners.[18] Japan has a timber building tradition normally associated with a frame structure and infill panels. However, specialist log buildings were constructed for the storage of precious things. The azekura was a structure raised off the ground with walls of logs cut in triangular cross-section. In the rainy season these would swell to keep out the rain and in cooler weather shrink to allow the air to flow through and around the stored treasures.[19] In the southern hemisphere, early settlers in Australia built houses from horizontal notched logs, such as the fine example with notched-log chimney in the Swan Hill Pioneer Settlement Museum in Victoria,[20] as well as huts with walls of vertical slabs, split from large logs, with the roof of stringy-bark tied to the rafters.[21] The Australian notched-log cabin is described as a crude building, one up from a tent.[22]

A log-building tradition generally arises in two ways. The first is because there are abundant forests and the climate, being cold, requires small, simple dwellings with few openings. These are the log-building traditions of northern

The exterior and interior of a Norwegian log house with a sod (turf) roof.

The exterior and interior of the Thomas Isaac one-roomed log cabin, built c.1780 and named after a nineteenth-century owner, now repositioned in Ellicott City near Baltimore.

Europe. The second, better related to Lincoln Logs, occurs in a newly settled land where the aim is to build a small secure house in a short time, with limited tools and materials. Log cabins are connected with the idea of pioneers establishing themselves in a new country, especially one in which – for those arriving from a more developed and depleted world – it would seem as if there were an endless supply of resources.[23] While timber was obviously valuable, trees were, conversely, often seen as a problem when it came to clearing the land for growing crops;[24] thus building with whole logs – not necessarily the most economical way to use timber – would not have mattered. Since the trees had to be cleared, the use of their trunks for house building was an obvious next step; it was like building with a 'waste' material.

The construction techniques may have come from northern European traditions (although, as shown, they had evolved separately in other parts of the world) but the log building is now associated with the spirit of the American pioneer. The log cabin was a humble starting point, but one that would be bettered with prosperity. Lincoln Logs did what the box lid claimed, in bringing 'to mind the early life of Abraham Lincoln' – the boy who rose from poverty to be President of the United States.[25] So important is this myth that a presidential hopeful in the 1950s attempted to boost support by referring to his birth in a log cabin in Oklahoma.[26]

The continuing popularity of Lincoln Logs probably has more to do with how Hollywood has portrayed frontier America in Western films rather than association with presidential aspirations. Lead cowboys and soldiers used to be sold to go with Lincoln Logs, and even modern sets come with accessory (plastic) toy cowboys and villains.[27] Lincoln Logs make the log cabin of the frontier town and the cowboy hero, exactly as depicted on the box lids.

A lot of words have been penned on the popularity of the Western, from examinations of Western film plots and how their implicit meanings are reflected in American institutions,[28] to the idea that the Western encapsulates the desire and fear of moving from adolescent to adult.[29] More recently, and perhaps more entertainingly, it has been suggested that Ronald Reagan adopted the same characters he had played in Westerns to gain and retain the presidency of the United States,[30] but with bigger guns to play with. However, it is doubtful that many of the thousands of children playing happily with Lincoln Logs have troubled their heads with structural analyses of their place in popular culture. A far more prosaic reason behind the popularity of the toy was the ritual of going to the Saturday matinee and seeing a Western serial, a staple for many children growing up in the decades between the 1930s and 1950s in the US.[31] Here they would have seen the log cabin set against the vast sky and open landscape of the Hollywood West, such as in the 1953 movie *Shane*. This classic Western involves the outsider hero of the title riding in to take the side of the settlers, whose log cabin homesteads and fields have been threatened by a cattle baron wanting the land for his free-ranging steers.[32]

Screen heroes such as Shane provided the fuel for another week of playing cowboy games, including some 'quiet' time playing with construction toys. Even the recent *Toy Story* series of movies has continued to cement the idea that the Western cowboy doll hero (Woody) will still be the one to save the day, even in the face of modern technology (the plastic Buzz Lightyear). The very realism of Lincoln Logs buildings and the fact they were fast to put together and relatively stable once made, so that games could be conducted around them, also contributed to their popularity. Their commercial success is confirmed by the number of near copies spawned in both the US and other countries.

One copy, American Logs, had squared wooden notched logs finished to look as if marked by an axe, and a different system of roof construction, presumably to avoid patent infringements. The fact that the roof gables were finished with triangular pieces made for a much better fit, but the underlying principle of building with horizontal notched logs was the same. Instructions were found on the reverse of the box lid, including an image of a Sawmill and Runway that leaves much to the imagination, since few children were likely to be familiar with this piece of industrial equipment. The final injunction among the images of cabins and sheds is to 'Buy more sets and build a complete frontier town.' So in addition to the pioneer image on the lid, the link with the Wild West town was not overlooked.

More powerful evidence for the argument that the success of these log cabin toys depended on the portrayal of the American West to children comes from two sets made and sold in New Zealand. New Zealand has, and maintains, a tradition of timber house building. Houses with walls of solid interlocking rectangular 'logs' are still made and sold under the Lockwood system,[33] which first appeared in 1953,[34] and most New Zealand children playing with the toy log cabins would have grown up in timber-frame houses. However, this tradition is never reflected or mentioned with these sets. The first, Logge and Timba, made in Auckland, was a very near copy of Lincoln Logs, despite the latter's patent,

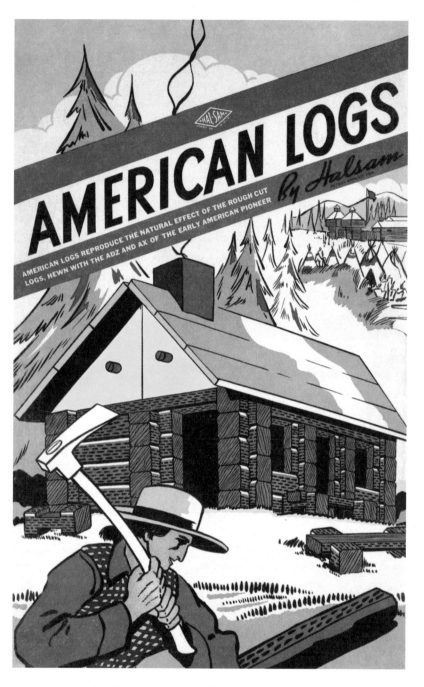

Pioneer imagery on the box lid of a set of American Logs.

with a slight variation in the triangular gable end and roof support arrangement. It came with a rather poorly printed parts list and pictures of various models, including the Kentucky cabin that was Abraham Lincoln's birthplace, a pioneer cabin, ranch house, schoolhouse and block house. The larger buildings that could be built with the 'De Luxe' set are shown surrounded by toy figures, including farm animals, a cowboy on a rearing horse, men with rifles and others (possibly Native Americans) firing bows and arrows. The second set by Jomax, called – wait for it – Log Cabin, has rectangular notched logs, some of which are grooved to hold the edges of the printed cardboard doors and curtained windows. It has a roof system directly copied from the French toy JeuJura (see below). The box has the slogan 'Build Miniature Pioneer Homes' and it also references the Western myth by giving each finished model with its parts list a name like 'Daniel Boone' and 'Davy Crocket' (sic).

One exception to the link between the marketing of log cabin construction toys and the Wild West might seem to be the 1946 French toy JeuJura, on which the New Zealand Log Cabin set was based. JeuJura had interlocking square logs and wooden roof sheets threaded onto purlins that fitted into notched gable pieces. The JeuJura kits are still available and make various European chalet-style buildings, complete with windows with working shutters.[35] When first produced, however, kits for both Western-style log cabins and European chalets were made.[36] So even in this very French version the log cabin still looked to the American West.

There was once a wide and rich tradition of building horizontal log buildings. Nor were these just confined to small one-roomed cabins and sheds, even in the US. Two-storey log-walled houses were built in towns and other settlements until the middle of the nineteenth century.[37] Solid log houses are still made, and often sold for rural and holiday living.[38] Yet it was not this tradition that toys like Lincoln Logs and its many followers offered, although the building technique exactly mimicked how such buildings are fundamentally constructed, which is a rare feature in construction toys. Lincoln Logs have long enjoyed popularity as a toy despite their limited range of buildings compared to sets of blocks, such as Richter, or even systems including Bayko (see Chapter 8).

Lincoln Logs make very good log cabin structures, but models are less convincing the further they stray from these simple buildings. At the core of their appeal are three ideas. The first is the patriotic link to the homes of the forefathers of America, reflected in both the name of the product and what it builds.

This was a move that was (and probably still is) going to make them popular with parents wishing to bring their children up as good Americans. The second idea is more romantic. Here the toy makes the pioneer dream: 'The cabin in the forest, on the banks of a quiet lake or buried in the wilderness back of beyond, is an expression of man's desire to escape the exactions of civilization and secure rest and seclusion by a return to the primitive.'[39] This is the cabin the writer and philosopher Henry David Thoreau constructed, and which formed his simple home for a number of years, although Thoreau talks of his hut in terms of cutting and hewing wood, and shaping rafters and studs, with the whole clad in weather boards.[40] The emphasis here is on simplicity, ensured because the cabin is self-built from the materials closest at hand and with the fewest possible tools. Time here is never an issue. This is what the small log homes of the past suggest, a lost satisfaction with having enough. This may go some way, again, to suggesting reasons why the toy appeals to adults, who are after all the ones with the big money. However, unlike Richter's blocks, adults are never shown playing with Lincoln Logs or similar toys on the box lids or in the instructions.

The toy had such lasting appeal for children quite simply because it reflected the West of fiction and film, of cowboys, Indians, cattle ranchers and home-steaders. It built a place where a pretend Laura Ingalls Wilder could explore the prairie from her little house, or somewhere for the Roy Rogers of the imagi-nation to play out the game of winning the West for freedom and democracy, before riding off into the sunset. Lincoln Logs are not so much a construction toy as proof that a really good story never tires in the telling.

CHAPTER SEVEN

Mobaco
and
De Stijl

D UTCH ARCHITECTURE IS KNOWN FOR ITS BRICKWORK, from the bond named after it (Dutch Bond: very common in solid walls, with an alternate header and stretcher in each row) to the 1920s brick expressionist housing schemes of Michel de Klerk and Piet Kramer, where brickwork forms the unlikely curved turrets and excrescences of what became known as the Amsterdam School.[1] However, when it comes to construction toys, the one from Holland that turns up all over the world is made of cardboard panels that slide into grooved wooden uprights. A continuous framework or grid, within which buildings are formed by inserting solid panels for the walls and roof, links this Dutch toy with the ideas of another Dutch movement, De Stijl.

Mobaco is a charmingly low-key toy, mostly of good-quality cardboard. You start with a fibreboard base with a grid of square holes in which you stand grooved upright wooden posts with chamfered tops. Cardboard panels of various types can then be slid between them, topped with horizontal card elements as ties and separators. The buildings are not stable without the cardboard inserts, but because these are quite large, the process is quick and a satisfactory structure soon results. In this it is unlike Bayko (see Chapter 8), which takes a similar approach but is much more trying on the temper.

The small house illustrated overleaf[2] is typical of what Mobaco makes. Almost all possible models in the instructions are buildings, apart from a bridge

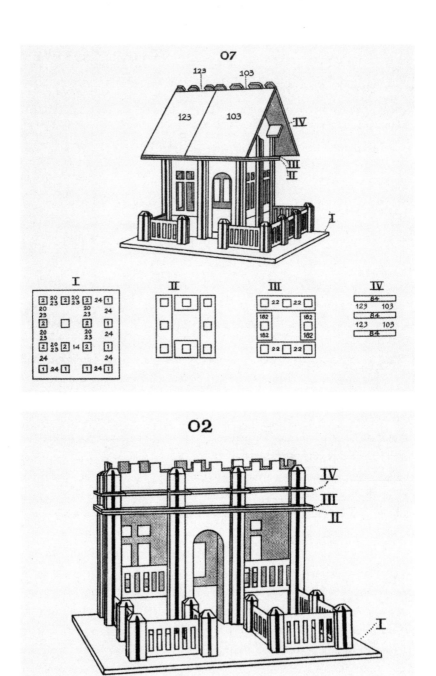

Extracts from a Mobaco instruction book showing a small pitched-roof house and a castellated building.

in the 1960s Jumbo-Spelen version of the toy. Somewhat surprisingly, given its Dutch origin, there are no plans for a windmill, although apparently there was an extremely rare special windmill set.[3] A modern all-wooden and uncoloured Mobaco is now made by Miniplex.[4] In original Mobaco, the base panel is uncoloured brown fibreboard, although later sets had dyed green bases; the wooden uprights were uncoloured and the cardboard inserts were variously grey, green, red and white with white gables and red interlocking roof panels. The instructions included many models with flat roofs, which could be given castellated parapets. Fence components meant that the area immediately outside the building was also part of the overall design and, in the later Jumbo sets, cardboard tree canopies could be slotted over the wooden uprights to complete the landscaping around the building.

The scale of the Mobaco models, determined by the window and door elements, conveniently fits that of the much later plastic Playmobil figures, also a toy with a Dutch connection. At the 1974 Nuremberg Toy Fair, a Dutch firm bought the complete first year's supply of this new German plastic toy.[5] Mobaco, however, is a Dutch invention, though its relationship with Dutch architecture is not obvious. It was a wooden and cardboard toy, made by a sheet metal firm (van Mouwerik and Bal in Zeist, near Utrecht[6]), in a country where timber buildings are rare. In addition, Dutch brick architecture is recognized as an important influence on building design, from the Elizabethan manor house[7] to the modern movement.[8] However, two architectural links will be explored here: the use of wood frames and infill brick panels in traditional houses; and the connection between sliding architectural elements and flexible architecture.

Renowned for their ingenuity, the Dutch not only created land from the sea, but also made houses out of window frames. Large areas of glazing seem very Dutch, not only because of the light-filled interiors of painters such as de Hooch and Vermeer, but also because of the way they form the outer framework of many buildings. Completely timber houses may be rare in the Netherlands, but substantial frames – kozijn – typically made from 100 x 125 mm- (4 x 5 in.) thick seasoned oak, often formed the structural skeleton of the house, with infill of brick or window sashes. You can see this in seventeenth-century Amsterdam houses with their gables facing the canals.[9] The lower storeys, often used as shop fronts or warehouses, would be of frame construction, with brick walls for the upper storeys or gables built on top of these.[10] This idea of frame with infill is retained even when the later construction is obviously brick. The façade is generated by a grid of closely spaced large windows; it is not merely a brick wall with openings. Suddenly the similarity between an architectural pattern and what could be made with Mobaco, especially some of the larger models, becomes clear.

The vertically sliding sash window is a possible precursor for the sliding elements of Mobaco. Further links emerge, as the counterbalanced vertically sliding sash window has been claimed as a Dutch invention by British scholars (and, with an unusual show of mutual respect, as a British invention by their Dutch counterparts).[11] Others suggest both parties are wrong and that the sash window first appeared at the end of the seventeenth century in France, since 'sash' is derived from the French word for frame, 'chassis'.[12] In the end it really does not matter. The Dutch, like the British, have used a lot of vertically sliding sash windows in their buildings, so it is interesting, though impossible to prove a connection, that two important sliding construction toys emanate from the Netherlands and Britain – Mobaco and Bayko.[13] Of the two, the Dutch toy is an elegant system that makes models only superficially similar to buildings children would see, whereas the English one is a complex and rather pragmatic system that makes quite accurate replicas of very familiar buildings.

Parallels, though not obvious at first, can be drawn between Mobaco and De Stijl. Founded in 1917 by Theo van Doesburg,[14] this artistic movement sought to create an abstraction of the world into its simplest elements: form and colour. Form started and ended with the rectangular grid, and colour with the three paint primaries of red, blue and yellow (not often found in building materials). As expressed in the paintings of Mondrian, with their grid of black lines on white and partial infilling of primary colours, the result is so instantly recognizable and iconic that it has even been used for high fashion clothes[15] and very expensive handbags.[16] However, because of this simplification, when it comes to three-dimensional works there are few examples. Two of the most important are both by Gerrit Rietveld, also an early member of the De Stijl group: the 1918 red-blue chair and the 1924 Schröder House in Utrecht. This house has been described as the only true De Stijl building.[17]

At first sight the house seems to have little to do with Mobaco apart from the fact that they both appeared in the early 1920s. However, the internal layout of the upper floor, devised by Rietveld to accommodate the wishes of the owner, Truus Schröder, depended on a series of sliding partitions that allowed the single space to be divided up in different ways to create enclosure, echoing the partitions and endless versatility of Mobaco's frames and sliding panels. The upper floor with central staircase had a bath and WC; it could be left as an open-plan space, or divided to form a landing with two bedroom areas and living/dining room, and a further small bedroom could be partitioned from the living area. Sliding doors also gave out onto balconies on the three exposed sides of the house (the back wall was against an existing terrace of houses). This arrangement gave rooms for Schröder's son (the small bedroom) and two girls (one bedroom area), while she finished up in the remaining bedroom with the grand piano for company. The partitions were carefully concealed when open by either sliding into a recess or folding against a fixed partition. (These sliding walls were left off the drawings submitted for approval because they contravened the regulations.[18]) Unlike Mobaco, where the elements slide in fixed grooves, the Schröder house partitions do not sit as elegantly on the grid when open as when folded, since the longer ones open in a staggered configuration.[19] The purity of concept exempli-fied in the toy is lost in the practicality of making the house work.

Perhaps of more significance for Mobaco is the De Stijl idea that the city was a continuum – the house was not a private box but an interior bounded by planes that linked the inside to the outside, just as the house owner or user was not sepa-rate from the city but a part of the whole urban population.[20] It is this intrinsic link between the inside and the outside space that is entrenched in the simple pierced Mobaco elements. Despite their seemingly conventional forms as windows and doors, the models have a transparency that allows views through in many directions. The sliding Mobaco panels merely punctuate this spatial con-tinuum, defined by the grid of wooden uprights. This idea of looking into and through windows has been noted as a 'unique cultural pattern'.[21] Being able to see inside houses and apartment blocks at night through large un-curtained windows, for instance, is something found in the Netherlands but not in her immediate neighbour, Germany, where the curtains will be firmly closed against onlookers when it gets dark.

A similar transparency can be seen with another important De Stijl building by J. J. P Oud, the Café De Unie in Rotterdam.[22] Although destroyed by bombs in the Second World War, it has since been rebuilt in another part of Rotterdam. The all-glass façade, with its essential primary colours, allows a clear view of the interior at street level. Oud was a co-founder of De Stijl with van Doesberg, and although he left the group over artistic differences in 1920, his work remains suggestive of the openness and skeletal quality of other Dutch modernists.[23]

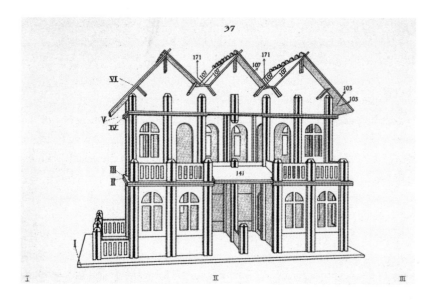

Instructions for a multi-gabled house in Mobaco (top) compared with typical Dutch gabled houses in Hoorn, The Netherlands.

Houses by architect Gerrit Rietveld in Utrecht: the 1924 Schröder House on Prins Hendriklaan, (top) and the 1927 Chauffeur's House, Waldeck Pyrmontkade 20.

The closest De Stijl building to Mobaco in terms of assembly technique is Rietveld's later design, the 1927 Chauffeur's House in Utrecht. This used a system of steel I-beam uprights with precast concrete panels slotted between them, the whole finished with a flat roof and based on a 1 x 1 metre module. Somehow, despite the Mobaco-like construction, the lack of transparency or through views takes this little house further from both Mobaco and De Stijl; in fact Rietveld left the group by 1928.

Mobaco connects with other Dutch architectural ideas. Dutch housing architecture has been characterized as anti-monumental, collective and modular,[24] and modularity is the first step to flexibility. The Netherlands is a country that fought to reclaim from the sea much of the land on which it is built. The high value thus placed on land suggests its buildings are never seen as permanent, but rather something to be changed in response to the emergence of new needs within society,[25] whether through renovation, demolition and starting again, or simply by moving internal partitions. In the hands of designers this led to the establishment of structures based on a grid, within which the house could be created. An example of this is a 1929 block of flats for the reasonably well-off built in The Hague. The potential occupants of Nirwana Flats could decide how much floor space they wanted within the reinforced concrete shell and how the apartment was to be laid out.[26] In other flats, sliding doors and foldaway beds made three-bedroom living possible in 51 square metres (550 sq ft).[27]

The reaction to this idea of flexibility based on design that used every square millimetre of available space came in 1961 from another Dutch architect, N. John Habraken. Worried by the appearance of high-rise blocks of flats, Habraken argued for housing to be focussed on the occupant rather than the designer or the building process. He proposed that basic 'supports' be provided within which each occupant could place their own infill 'units'. These units would be bought like other consumer goods.[28] In 1964 Habraken established SAR (translated as the Foundation for Architectural Research) and the principles were applied to the Lunetten residential district near Utrecht. This housing scheme echoes the Mobaco colours,[29] is philosophically based on the Mobaco principles of supports and infill, and is in the same city as the Mobaco factory and Rietveld's Schröder house. The Netherlands is not a large country, but this seems more than a coincidence. It is not far-fetched to think that Habraken might have played with Mobaco as a child.

72

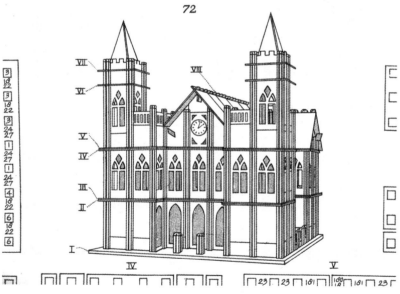

The Rijksmuseum in Amsterdam, by Pierre Cuypers built between 1876 and 1889 (top) and a Mobaco equivalent.

In his manifesto for a new Plastic Architecture, published in his magazine *De Stijl* in 1924, van Doesburg could be describing Mobaco. The new architecture was to be open, with connection between interior and exterior, and the internal layout had to have moveable partitions with no fixed party walls[30] (which would have formed some very challenging acoustic problems if your neighbours were not totally silent). However, Mobaco, as shown in the illustrations, did not produce the modernist flat-roof ideal house with its open plan and (perhaps) inevitable grand piano, but instead made rather charming buildings with a historic feel, more reminiscent of the work of the nineteenth-century Dutch architect Pierre Cuypers than the Dutch heroes of the modern movement.[31]

Yet the Zeitgeist, should such a thing exist, that produced the toy and the new architecture proclaimed in the pages of *De Stijl*, made manifest an idea that could be applied to either. In terms of their structure, Mobaco buildings are refreshingly clear and at the same time entirely satisfactory. This search for structural clarity has been described as a modernist goal.[32] They are also quick to make, another modernist dream that underpinned the drive to find the ideal method for prefabricating houses.

CHAPTER EIGHT

Bayko
and
Suburbia

A POSTWAR SYMBOL OF BRITAIN'S ABBEY NATIONAL BUILDING SOCIETY
was a young couple sheltering under an umbrella in the form of a red
hipped roof with chimney stack (a hipped roof has four downward-
sloping sides). Its designer, Eric Winter (1905–81), who illustrated many of the
Ladybird children's books, is quoted as saying that when he designed the logo in
the 1950s, he copied the roof of a house opposite his studio in the suburb of
Broxbourne.[1] A study of modern Broxbourne, near London, certainly shows
plenty of hipped-roof houses, demonstrating that it was a good choice as
a symbol of the suburbs. Similarly, it was the red plastic hipped roofs in the
Bayko box that guided the Bayko builder towards the construction of interwar
suburban Britain on the carpet – the very suburbia that the building societies,
Britain's mutually owned savings and loan organizations, helped to finance.

C. B. Plimpton, the inventor of Bayko, applied for a patent for it in 1933, and
it was marketed the following year by the newly established Plimpton Engineering
in Liverpool. Plimpton developed Bayko while convalescing from tuberculosis in
a sanatorium, and it is said to have been based on Mobaco.[2] Perhaps because of
Plimpton's illness, Bayko's instruction booklets have always emphasized hygiene:
'Bayko Sets are clean and hygienic; easily sterilized by placing in boiling water;
ideal toys for children incapacitated by sickness or disease.'[3] Sadly, despite
Bayko's hygienic qualities, Plimpton died of tuberculosis in 1948 at the age of

99

fifty-five. Unlike the cardboard and wood Mobaco, which would have made only an unsavoury broth if placed in boiling water, boilable Bayko was the first plastic construction set.[4] The original toys were called 'Bayko Light Construction Sets'. This title was probably a pun since they were first advertised (in the *British Plastics and Moulded Products Trader*) by Bakelite Ltd of London, who made the material out of which they were manufactured,[5] although 'light buildings' was also a term in use to describe buildings of non-traditional (particularly timber) construction.[6] Publicly announced in 1909, Bakelite is a thermosetting plastic, that is not distorted by heat (so you can boil it) and is made from phenol and formaldehyde. It was the first material to be made entirely by man. In 1993, Bakelite, named after its Belgian-born inventor Leo Hendrik Baekeland, was designated a National Historic Chemical Landmark by the American Chemical Society.[7] The original 'Bakelizer', the iron steam-punk-looking vessel in which the plastic was first manufactured, is now in the National Museum of American History in Washington, D. C.

Of all the construction sets discussed here Bayko is the most utterly perverse in the way it is put together. The other sets, in their various ways, imitate the process of construction. Block is piled upon block (albeit usually without mortar), or log is piled upon log, or beam is bolted to beam in an admittedly sometimes fairly vague imitation of the process employed on site. Even if the bricks are made of rubber, they still have to be bonded and lintels must be used to span openings. The Bayko builder, on the other hand, begins construction by fixing together a number of green Bakelite bases, each 3¾ x 5¼ inches (9.5 x 13 cm), using little metal links and screws, and a tiny Bayko screwdriver with a (presumably) Bakelite handle. These bases are covered with a grid of holes, spaced ⅜ inch (9.5 mm) apart, and into these holes you have to insert thin steel rods of different lengths, following the line of where the walls of the proposed building are to be. The rods have to be the same length as the desired wall height – difficult if you are designing a complex building, as, if you get it wrong, it is not usually possible to pull the rods out and change them halfway through construction without precipitating a total collapse. Grooved Bakelite wall panels, coloured either red or white from 1939 onwards, and incised to represent bricks, are slid between the metal rods, provided that the builder has managed not to bend the rods in trying to get them fixed into the holes in the base. Not bending the rods is quite a challenge, as they are both thin and a tight fit in the holes. You slide windows and doors into the growing building in the same way.

A Bayko box lid image showing a typical interwar suburban house and garage, somewhat exaggerated in size compared to the dimensions of the true Bayko model.

The whole structure is not at all stable until thin sheet-steel corner ties and continuous sheet-steel tie bars are added to the top of the walls to bind together the protruding ends of the rods. These ties are quite easy to bend or break.

If more than a single-storey building is required, intermediate floors made of Paxolin, a phenolic-paper laminate[8] (in other words, something like paper impregnated with Bakelite) are fitted to provide some much-needed racking resistance. The floors are paper-thin and have the same grid of holes as the bases – fitting them over the protruding rods requires a great deal of patience to avoid destroying the floor. If the rods are at all bent, the problem is greatly compounded. However, when completed, the Bayko building is quite solid and much less easy to knock over than one made of Lott's Bricks. This is an important point, especially for buildings you might use with toy trains. Finally, a pre-formed hipped red Bakelite roof (small, medium or large) is dropped onto the walls to complete the effect. These roofs, in three sizes, are in many ways the defining component of Bayko. They express interwar suburbia with utter precision; at the same time they determined the depth of the boxes in which the sets are sold – so much so that the boxes contained a series of cardboard platforms to fill up some of the space and present the remaining parts more effectively.

One of the biggest changes made when Bayko was taken over by Meccano in 1960[9] was the abandonment of the preformed hipped roofs and their replacement with a full range of flat roof panels, two of which could be used with separate gable ends to form a fairly shallow pitched roof. Apart from changing the architectural style of Bayko to something more like the suburbs of the sixties, this move also made the boxes much thinner and much more like the boxes that Meccano Outfits came in at that time.

Despite the strangely complex technology and construction process, which seem so much more suitable for a *machine à habiter* (Le Corbusier's phrase: a machine for living in) than a suburban villa, the models that can be made from Bayko are totally recognizable as part of suburban Britain, whether a Seaside Shelter (Set No. 0) that could be in Worthing, or a pair of semi-detached houses with attached garages (Set No. 3) that could be anywhere from Basildon to Wythenshaw.

The classic big blue Bayko boxes of the 1950s show an archetypal suburban image of the large hipped-roof House with Garage. Playing with it are two nicely dressed children, the boy wearing a tie while the girl watches admiringly and clutches her rather dissolute-looking doll. Unlike Meccano, there is no pipe-smoking father looking on approvingly at the model his children (boys only, of course, on the Meccano Manual, and both wearing ties) have created, but at least Bayko does show a model to which you could aspire. The big House and Garage can be made from the Bayko Set No. 4, (it is the first model in the instruction book for that set), although the box does show balcony components that were never marketed, and it appears to be missing one of its dormer windows.

It is conjectured by the Bayko enthusiast and historian Pete Bradley (aka the Baykoman), that nearly 10% of households in the UK had a Bayko set during the thirty years that it was produced.[10] In total, nearly two million sets were manufactured. Many were owned by suburban families who would have felt at home in Bayko's creation of an instantly recognizable world. There were Bayko garages for the cars so essential to suburban living, and the instruction books show many examples of buildings that would form part of the suburban family's annual holiday when they took the car to the seaside, including the Seaside Chalet (Set No. 1), Promenade Café (Set No. 2) and Pier Pavilion (Set No. 3). En route they might stop at the Wayside Café (Set No. 0) or the Milk Bar (Set No. 2), or, if wealthy enough to own Set No. 3, it might be the rather more louche Road House.

Unlike Meccano, which has its declared adherents, few architects seem to have played with Bayko, or, if they did, they have kept quiet about it. One exception is the Canadian architecture academic and author Witold Rybczynski, who gives a detailed account of playing with Bayko, describing its red and white wall panels, the green windows and the hipped roofs. Rybczynski, however, initially claims not to remember what it was called, although he remembers playing with both Meccano and Canadian Logs (like Lincoln Logs)[11] by name. Rybczynski defines the style of Bayko as postwar contemporary,[12] which seems very implausible, since it is much more readily described, as suggested above, as interwar suburban. Admittedly some Bayko components were redesigned and the colours changed when it was taken over by Meccano in 1960, giving a slightly more 'postwar contemporary' look, but Rybczynski describes playing with red and white Bayko with green windows, so he is talking about the classic version, not the later one. However, he is not necessarily an expert on construction toys, since he claims that Lott's Bricks were 'cut from Italian marble.'[13] Interestingly, in a book written three years later, Rybczynski managed to remember Bayko by name, and described how he watched his father and uncle building a garden shed

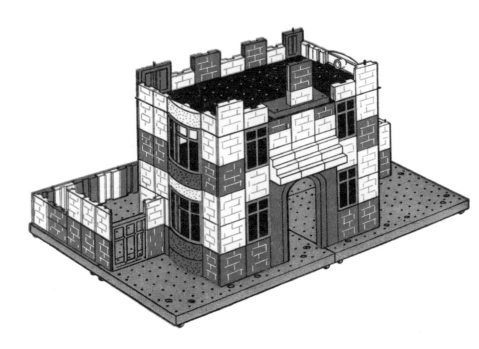

Part of the instructions for making a Road House in Bayko; the pattern embossed on the plastic wall pieces is brick and there is a pebble-dash finish below the bay window, both typical components of interwar suburban building in the UK.

using a system of precast concrete panels slid down between uprights that reminded him of the toy.[14]

It is possible to surmise that architects now prefer not to remember Bayko, because it was so determinedly suburban, and the suburbs stand for everything that architects are taught to dislike. Indeed, the possible reason that an architect's education takes seven years is that it takes that long to learn to despise everything that other people like. Architects have long tended to have a rather dim view of the suburbs, summed up in modern architecture's *Athens Charter* as 'one of the greatest evils of the century.'[15] Given this castigation of the suburbs was written a few months after Adolf Hitler became Chancellor of Germany, the architects might have been guilty of a very slight exaggeration.

The *Athens Charter*, like much disparagement of suburban architecture, emanated from a privileged, even patrician milieu. It was a manifesto written mostly by Le Corbusier to summarize the 1933 Fourth Congress of the International Congresses of Modern Architecture (Congrès Internationaux d'Architecture Moderne, CIAM). He founded CIAM in 1928 with the historian Sigfried Giedion and other modernist architects who were upset at what they considered unfair treatment (i.e. not winning) in the competition to design a new headquarters in Geneva for the League of Nations.[16] They were sponsored initially by a French-Swiss noblewoman, Hélène de Mandrot, and met at her chateau near Geneva.[17] The members of CIAM then continued their engagement with the less fortunate by discussing the 'Functional City' in the agreeable surroundings of a Mediterranean cruise.

They hammered out their vision for the future of the urban working masses at their Fourth Congress, aboard the *Patris II* sailing from Marseille to Piraeus, Athens and back over two weeks. This ship had accommodation for a hundred first class passengers and a hundred and fifty second class, as well as 'deck passengers'.[18] History does not record how the approximately one hundred CIAM delegates[19] travelled, but it is hard to imagine Le Corbusier, László Moholy-Nagy, Sigfried Giedion, Ernö Goldfinger, Wells Coates, Fernand Léger, Charlotte Perriand, Otto Neurath[20] and their chums going as deck passengers, or even second class. Their comments about suburbs had a wide influence: the *Athens Charter*, which recorded the decisions made at the Fourth Congress (or cruise), has been credited with being the blueprint for urban development after the Second World War in Europe, the United States, the Communist world and many developing countries around the globe.[21]

Peckham Library, south London, completed in 2000 and designed by Will Alsop, an architect who remembers playing with Bayko.

This jaundiced but prevalent view of suburbia is seen also in a report on a 1993 exhibition of building toys at RIBA (Royal Institute of British Architects) in London, which relates that architect Will Alsop made lots of Bayko buildings as a child.[22] The journalist describes as 'rather ugly' the 1930s suburban houses that you could build with Bayko. Alsop's buildings are superficially nothing like Bayko, but his use of slender columns at various angles to support both the Peckham Library, London (2000), and the Sharp Centre for Design in Toronto (2004) does undeniably recall the Bayko rods, and particularly how they tended to bend when inserted into the base too vigorously. Maybe Bayko was more influential than it at first appears.

In a letter to the *RIBA Journal*, another architect describes building 'noddy-style houses' (sic) in Bayko as a boy in the 1950s.[23] Architects often write without really understanding their material: Noddy and his Toyland world are in fact extremely interesting architecturally. In *Noddy Goes to Toyland*,[24] Noddy is actually bought, by his new friend Big-Ears, a self-build House-for-One package (thus predating IKEA by 60 years[25]) on credit from a large housing supply depot in Toyland, which he and Big Ears assemble on a squatted vacant site with help from Noddy's new neighbours, a couple of bears – not at all the typical suburban dream. The neighbouring vernacular dwellings in Toytown are over-crowded, prompting Noddy's need to create his own housing solution. Architecturally, Noddy's house is quite radically postmodern compared to his neighbours', built as it is from pale green, yellow and pink bricks, with a portico supported on squat columns and a red roof. Big-Ears' house is built of bio-materials, making him a very green Toylander. The Dutch illustrator of the first Noddy books, Harmsen van der Beek,[26] could be credited with inventing post-modernism and Green Architecture. It is also pleasing to note that before drawing Noddy he drew the illustrations for the prewar Mobaco sets, showing cheerful gnomes (*kabouters* in Dutch) looking very like Big-Ears, carrying build-ing materials, going to the market, or rushing to catch a train.

It would appear that many in the architectural profession have a profound dislike of the sorts of suburbia in which many of them were probably born and raised. Modernist J. M. Richards acknowledged as much in his 1946 book *Castles on the Ground*.[27] In spite of its completely alien technology, Bayko recreates this suburban experience. Interestingly, Bayko could also be used to build the white cubes of modernism. There are certainly white bricks. What it lacks are suitably modern windows. However, a firm called Transport of Delight now makes a

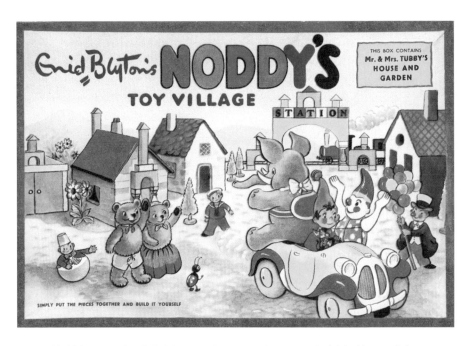

Noddy's postmodern kit-built house and garage can be seen on the left in this general view of Toytown housing.

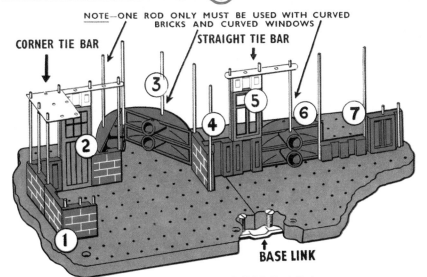

METHODS OF USING 𝐁𝐀𝐘𝐊𝐎 PARTS

NOTE—ONE ROD ONLY MUST BE USED WITH CURVED BRICKS AND CURVED WINDOWS

CORNER TIE BAR

STRAIGHT TIE BAR

BASE LINK

1. Corner made by using End Brick with ordinary Brick.
2. Door plus Half Brick equals three Bricks in height.
3. Commencement of Full Bay Window; note wires are placed through the OUTSIDE hole ONLY.
4. Method of interlocking Bricks.
5. Brick, Window and Half Brick equals three Bricks in height.
6. Commencement of Small Bay Window; note wires are placed through the INSIDE hole ONLY.
7. Long Brick, two of which are equal in length to three Bricks.

Bayko instructions for fitting pieces together, showing how strange and complex the building method was.

kind of improved Bayko: 'BAYKO MASTER PLANS – *all the enjoyment of archi-tecture with none of the risk, expense and mess of the real thing'*. These plans, which include a modern, white 'Chauffeur/Gardener's Lodge' and a Charles Holden-style Underground station,[28] make use of new Bayko components created by Brian Salter under the name Bayko 2000, which provide appropriate forms of doors and windows. Originally Bayko also made 'wall cappings', which allowed the young architect to cover up the protruding ends of the rods and form a parapet on a flat-roofed building, but these useful parts were discontinued in 1939. It can be assumed from this that Bayko was not intended to be used to produce modern building forms, even though it could do this quite well. It was determinedly and deliberately connected to the suburbs. In contrast, Lott's Bricks managed to supply horizontal modern steel windows in later sets and, as described earlier, model railways pushed modernist buildings.

No doubt Bayko's lack of interest in the modern is at least partly because Charles Plimpton was not a member of the Design and Industries Association, and had no architectural axe to grind. He, not unreasonably, was offering his customers a building set that made models of the buildings around them. Fascinatingly, he did this through advanced materials (Bakelite) and a prefab-ricated construction technology that was quite unlike anything out there in the real world.

CHAPTER NINE

Minibrix
and Unassuming
Architecture

M INIBRIX HAS BEEN DESCRIBED AS A RUBBER VERSION OF LEGO, but that rather undervalues this toy, because it makes much more realistic-looking buildings. Whereas modern plastic Lego makes houses in a range of saturated primary colours, a wall of dyed rubber Minibrix looks like a wall of brickwork somewhere (anywhere) in Britain, though perhaps on a wet day. And with Minibrix you can make the buildings, good but perhaps unremarked, that you might also see anywhere in Britain.

First sold in 1935, Minibrix was another architectural toy initially marketed for boys – only boys make buildings on the original box lids, while on the lids of later sets the girl looks on with an awed wonder, with her hands firmly behind her back. The Minibrix club (Minibuilders) was something any boy with a set of Minibrix could join. It published a bulletin and boys were encouraged to send in their designs, which if published earned the sum of 5 shillings.[1] Unfortunately, this was not sufficient to buy a set of Minibrix, as the No. 2 set cost 10 shillings and sixpence in 1936[2] (roughly equivalent to £30 today). Girls were shown making models on the cover of the instruction manuals in the 1950s, but by this time the factory was already running into trouble – maybe that's why.

In Minibrix, each rubber brick fits into holes on the top of the brick below, the inverse of modern Lego. Angled bricks made gable ends. The finished models are heavier than Lego, making them more realistic in terms of mass for volume.

MODELS BUILT WITH 𝕿𝖚𝖉𝖔𝖗 SET 3

MODEL T3/I — MODEL OF YE OLDE HOSTEL OF GOD-BEGOT, WINCHESTER, HANTS

This old Tavern dates back to the 10th Century. The present building was constructed in 1558, and was at one time a manor, holding its own courts, a privilege that remained until the Dissolution of the Monasteries by Henry VIII. It is everywhere regarded as a wonderful example of Tudor architecture.

Parts required :

62 Whole bricks (black)	24 3-in. lintels (black)
226 Whole bricks (white)	10 3-in. lintels (white)
226 Half bricks (black)	117 Universal pins
209 Half bricks (white)	16 Bracing bricks
13 Angle bricks (black)	88 Whole tiles
54 Angle bricks (white)	18 Half tiles
6 1-in. lintels (black)	14 Whole ridge tiles
8 1-in. lintels (white)	3 Gothic doors
25 2-in. lintels (black)	6 Small windows
9 2-in. lintels (white)	3 Large windows
	6 6-in. purlins (angle section)

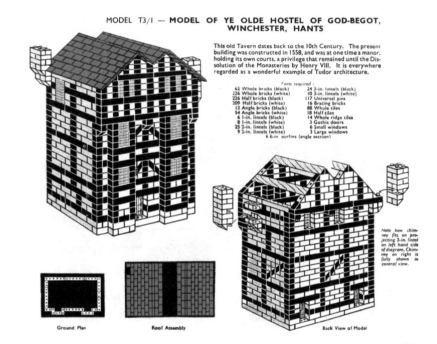

Note how chimney fits on projecting 3-in. lintel on left hand side of diagram. Chimney on right is fully shown in general view.

Ground Plan   Roof Assembly   Back View of Model

PATENTEES AND MANUFACTURERS, PREMO RUBBER CO. LTD., PETERSFIELD, HANTS. ENGLAND.

God Begot House in Winchester today (opposite), and instructions for building the former inn in Tudor Minibrix.

Doors and windows were included; these were printed on celluloid with tiny lugs that fitted into equally tiny holes in the rubber bricks, which could be quite fiddly. There were also rather bendy rubber lintels to go over the openings. Lintel-like bricks formed the foundation course, though later there were also base boards to build on. The whole system teaches much about the need for bonding brickwork. The roofs are like the Lott's Bricks design, being made of hinged green rubber plates embossed with a tile pattern. Other parts were soon added, such as short fluted cylinders that stacked to make Corinthian pillars and were also useful as chimney pots, and balustrades that could be bonded to the rest of the structure with tiny black rubber 'universal pins'; these were the first thing to get lost and it is now rare to find Minibrix sets complete with all of these.

Making models in old sets is not for the faint-hearted, though construction was relatively easy when the bricks were new. The rubber hardens with the years and considerable strength is needed to make the bricks interlock. But old rubber also sags under its own weight, so the roof plates, now, do not make for very convincing flat-roof buildings (or maybe this is convincing of a flat roof over time).

Minibrix were manufactured by the Premo Rubber Company of Petersfield in southern England, who made rubber heels for shoes under licence from the US. Minibrix was not the first of its kind. In 1934, the Rubber Specialities Company of Pennsylvania sold a studded rubber brick toy called Bild-O-Brik.[3] Arnold Levy, the owner of the Premo Rubber Company, made many trips to the US and he could have been inspired by Bild-O-Brik to diversify his business.[4] Later, black-and-white Tudor Minibrix were introduced, with new parts, including Gothic doors, larger windows, and triangular purlins on which the roofs were constructed from tiles, ridges and half versions of each. For once roofs were laid as they would be in the real world, from the eaves up to the ridge. Curious black rhomboidal bricks allowed the construction of diagonal bracing. These sets built replicas of well-known 'black-and-white' buildings, such as Anne Hathaway's Cottage, near Stratford, and the God Begot House in Winchester. Minibrix also produced large models of real buildings, including Buckingham Palace and the Empire State Building, for exhibition and shop display.[5] The latter, at 4 feet (1.2m) high, appeared on the cover of the early instruction books, although how the average family could afford, or even house, that many bricks is a mystery.

Ordinary Minibrix was sold with designs by 'the well known architect W. A. T. Carter A.R.I.B.A...'.[6] Whether this was intended to mirror the part Arnold Mitchell had played in Lott's Bricks is conjecture. Carter, however, was not as well known as Mitchell. He was a local Petersfield architect,[7] and probably designed the conversion of a barn in Liphook to a squash court and games room, a project published in 1914.[8] So unknown is Mr Carter that his obituary in the *Architect and Building News* did no more than regret his passing in 1941, with no mention of Minibrix.[9]

Given that Minibrix arrived a few years before the Second World War, the designs in the instructions show only a sporadic modern influence. Most are generic buildings, some of which could have drawn inspiration from Petersfield itself. The church built with Set 4 is like Petersfield Church of the late 1800s,[10] and the same town's market hall also resembles a Minibrix model. However, the Art Deco-inspired factory built with the No. 6 set is not an image of the modest Premo Rubber factory.[11] It better echoes factories designed by Wallis, Gilbert and Partner in west London.[12] This was a little-known firm who left their mark in terms of the design of factories and bus stations (Victoria Coach Station, 1931–32, for example). As such, they represent the breed of architects, such as Carter, who contribute much to the built environment but never achieve 'prima donna' status. These are the architects of local fire stations, public libraries and cowsheds, all of which appear as Minibrix models. Their buildings, like the Minibrix models, also tend to draw on their Arts and Crafts roots rather than modernist exemplars. Three of these hidden architects will be discussed here to show that, despite Nikolaus Pevsner's statement to the contrary,[13] a bicycle shed (actually we'll discuss cowsheds) in the right hands can be architecture.

Architects' names are often hidden when they move from private practice to work for a local council or government department. As a group these architects have received brickbats, with their work described in 1938 as 'stale chocolate'.[14] Charles Winmill falls into this category. In 1892 he joined the architects' department of the London County Council (LCC). A bad fire in the City of London in 1897 gave rise to a new fire station on Redcross Street,[15] and Winmill was put in charge of this. (It opened in 1900 but was destroyed in the Blitz.[16]) He was promoted in 1899 to become second-in-command of the fire-brigade section at the LCC, and for the next twenty-four years Winmill's architectural life was fire stations, even if he took inspiration for his designs from his beloved English churches,[17] for instance citing St Clement Danes

The 1929–30 Pyrene Building by Wallis, Gilbert and Partner, Great West Road, Brentford (above), compared with instructions for a factory in Minibrix.

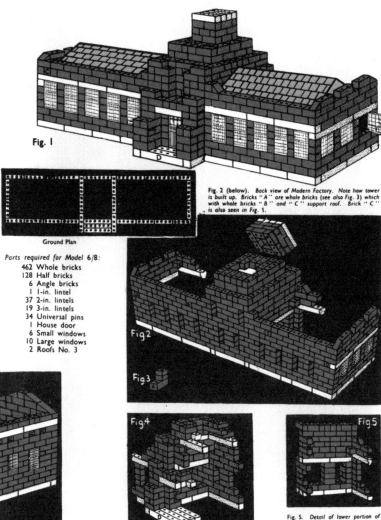

Fig. 1

Fig. 2 (below). Back view of Modern Factory. Note how tower is built up. Bricks "A" are whole bricks (see also Fig. 3) which with whole bricks "B" and "C" support roof. Brick "C" is also seen in Fig. 1.

Ground Plan

Parts required for Model 6/8:
462 Whole bricks
128 Half bricks
6 Angle bricks
1 1-in. lintel
37 2-in. lintels
19 3-in. lintels
34 Universal pins
1 House door
6 Small windows
10 Large windows
2 Roofs No. 3

Fig 2

Fig 3

Fig 4

Fig 5

Fig. 4. Half-section of Tower and front entrance to show interior construction. Lintel "D" in Fig. 1 and above drawing will identify exact position.

Fig. 5. Detail of lower portion of Tower wall inside building. Half brick "D" in above diagram and Fig. 4 serves to identify the exact position of this section.

as the inspiration for Redcross Street fire station, with a chimney stack instead of a spire.[18]

Fire stations usually come with towers for drying hoses, water storage or training. Architecturally this gives the opportunity for massing based on the tower and block. For a construction toy, a tower combined with a lower building is an interesting challenge, as anything involving differential massing is more complex. The first Minibrix fire station model is the Forest Fire Station in the 1941 manual. Architecturally it was a combination of a tower structure with a long, low accommodation block. Quite why there should be a Forest Fire Station is a mystery, since these were American rather than British. The North American fire lookout tower, usually without a fire station, was vital in preventing the spread of wildfires by spotting any smoke.[19] The only urban fire observation tower in the UK is in the Sheffield Fire and Police Museum in Yorkshire, which is the original, *c.*1900, Fire Station,[20] but this is not the inspiration for the Minibrix model. Perhaps this is evidence of a Minibrix connection with the American Bild-o-Brik toy.

When Winmill was designing his first fire stations, appliances were still drawn by horses, so stables and coachmen had to be accommodated. The fire service was motorized early in the twentieth century, although accommodation was often provided for the firemen and their families on site. The 1908 station in Tooting, south London, was the first motorized station, with the horses being 'handed over to the horse contractor,' which hopefully was not a euphemism for the glue factory.[21]

Winmill's architecture is encapsulated in his fire station on a wedge of land in Hampstead, north London, completed in 1915.[22] It was a fire station, hose drying tower and residential accommodation, drawing on the Arts and Crafts manner of earlier LCC fire stations, such as Perry Vale.[23] However, rather than picturesque Perry Vale's octagonal tower with a pyramidal roof balancing somewhat insecurely on the top,[24] the beautiful sparseness of Winmill's fire station has been controlled by his devotion to the Arts and Crafts architect Philip Webb. From Webb, Winmill drew the experience of handling materials both simply and respectfully. Sir John Summerson described the Hampstead fire station as simultaneously practical and sensitive, being the work of someone, 'like Philip Webb...', who understood the vernacular traditions of southern England.[25] Elsewhere, Summerson suggests that a sound knowledge of such traditions was the basis of early-twentieth-century functionalism (the view that design should

The Arts and Crafts-inspired Fire Station by LCC Fire Brigade Department, Perry Vale, 1901–2 (top), and the brick-built 1914–15 Forest Hill Fire Station, Hampstead, by Winmill, inspired by Philip Webb.

MODEL 5/1 - - - - - CENTRAL SCHOOL

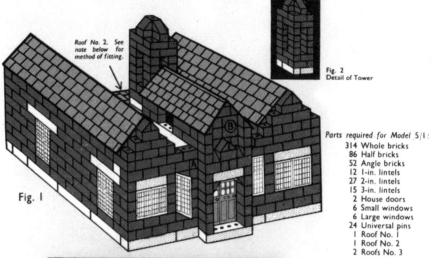

Roof No. 2. See note below for method of fitting.

Fig. 2
Detail of Tower

Fig. 1

Parts required for Model 5/1:
314 Whole bricks
86 Half bricks
52 Angle bricks
12 1-in. lintels
27 2-in. lintels
15 3-in. lintels
2 House doors
6 Small windows
6 Large windows
24 Universal pins
1 Roof No. 1
1 Roof No. 2
2 Roofs No. 3

Back view of Central School

NOTE—Fig. 4 shows interior construction of model with back wall cut away. The tower (Fig. 2) rests on a flat roof (No. 2) as seen in Fig 1. This roof rests between the back wall and the two bricks (" A ") built out from the front wall, as seen in Figs. 1 and 4. This roof also fits underneath and supports the back of roof section (" B ").

Ground Plan

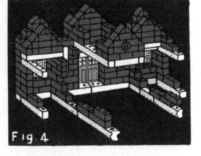

Fig. 4

A Minibrix School (opposite) and a 1912 painting by James Mackenzie of Barrington Colliery School; the colours are reversed, but the spirit is the same.

reflect purpose).[26] It is also the ordinariness of these traditions that make the link with Minibrix. A very simple mix of materials and elements are skilfully combined to give an exceptional but well-mannered result, which is the essence of good vernacular building. Winmill might be amused to know that his Hampstead fire station is now Grade II* listed.[27]

Another local government architect was George Topham Forrest, a Scot who headed the LCC Architects Department in 1919. Before then he had worked on schools in Yorkshire and was County Education Architect for Northumberland, where in 1906 his salary of £250 came with an annual £9 bicycle allowance[28] – truly the days when architects were real architects. Topham Forrest began his school design career in rural areas, where the school was an important part of village life. The 1941 Minibrix manual contains instructions for such a village school, but curiously this is flat-roofed with Gothic doors, rather than the normal pitched roof. Small schools go with elementary education, which spread in the Victorian era.[29] Many were established by the church, so it is no surprise the buildings were usually clothed in a striped Gothic style.[30] The flat roof, however, belongs to a much later era of school design and is more typically American than British,[31] again pointing to possible American antecedents for the Minibrix models. The modernist flat-roofed school appeared in the US in 1929,[32] and by the mid-1930s examples were also appearing in Britain – though not with Gothic windows and a classical pediment over the front door (perhaps not Minibrix's finest architectural moment).

Minibrix also had an imposing Central School[33] with tower and classrooms either side. This was a school arrangement again dating back to the nineteenth century.[34] Topham Forrest's 1912 Barrington Colliery School in Northumberland has a similar feel to the Minibrix models, though it is not the same. It is a simple gabled building with bright green wooden walls and red asbestos roof, the colour inverse of Minibrix. Notably his design was an innovative response to the need for a lightweight building in mining areas prone to subsidence.[35] This was one of a series of Topham Forrest schools for rural areas, in timber and galvanized iron, all with cross ventilation to ensure a good indoor atmosphere. Although cheap, Barrington Colliery School was sufficiently robust to last until 1949,[36] around the time the colliery closed.[37]

Topham Forrest used this early experience to formulate his approach to school-building. In an article of 1924 he wrote that it was not possible to design the ideal school building as educational theories were always changing. He advocated classrooms built of semi-permanent materials so they could be easily altered as educational approaches varied.[38] One educational theory he used in his LCC designs was that of the open-air schools. This movement began at the start of the twentieth century in Germany and spread rapidly in Europe and the US.[39] Its effect was to make sure all classrooms had good cross ventilation and plenty of daylight, with glazed doors that could be opened out to verandas.[40] Classroom blocks thus became long and thin, as reflected in the Minibrix Central School. The same principles were used by Topham Forrest in 1928 for an unusual three-storey primary school in Ealdham Square, Greenwich, in southeast London, where the glazed doors opened out onto a narrow balcony with wrought-iron railings on the upper floors.[41] Topham Forrest and architects like him were aware of the importance of school design for the developing child, and the care they gave to these buildings, usually anonymously, is a shining example of architecture in the service of the people.

Minibrix gives instructions for farm buildings, including a cowshed and a farmhouse: solid, very British-looking buildings that reflected the very ordinariness of their real-life counterparts. One architect whose career was partly involved with farm buildings was Edwin Gunn, who worked with a team of architects at the Ministry of Agriculture and Fisheries after the First World War on a scheme to provide land for smallholdings for ex-service men. Design was also to play a part in the revival of agriculture. For the farmer to compete against cheap imports, smallholdings had to use the most efficient husbandry.[42] At the time Gunn retired in 1934, he had control of all Ministry building work 'in Southern England below the Humber and Trent.'[43] One major task was the adaptation and erection of new houses and farm buildings on the major part of the huge Sutton Bridge estate in Lincolnshire. Because Gunn also designed houses and became an author and inveterate writer of letters to the journals, in particular *The Architect and Building News*, his name is not often associated with the Ministry buildings he designed.

Just as open-air schools had embraced the outside as being good for health, similar ideas were developed for housing farm animals. In his 1935 book *Farm Buildings: New and Adapted*, Gunn argued for fresh air without draughts, and sufficient insulation in the walls and roof of the cowshed or other building for stock to avoid excessive heat loss in winter and heat gain in summer; heat loss would result in having to feed more in the winter, and too much heat in summer led to loss of condition.[44]

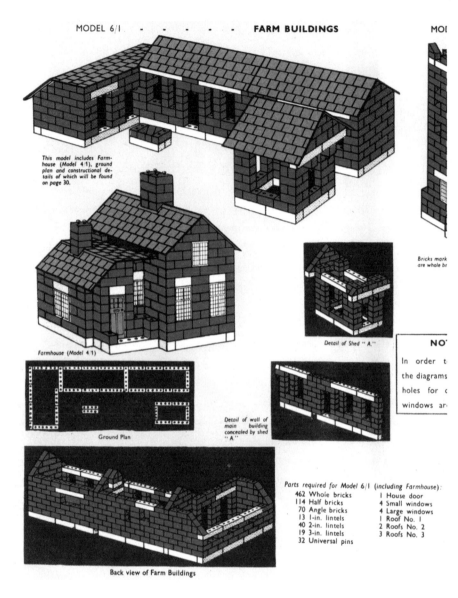

This model includes Farmhouse (Model 4/1), ground plan and constructional details of which will be found on page 30.

Farmhouse (Model 4/1)

Ground Plan

Detail of Shed " A."

Detail of wall of main building concealed by shed " A."

Bricks mark
are whole br

NO

In order t
the diagrams
holes for c
windows ar

Back view of Farm Buildings

Parts required for Model 6/I (including Farmhouse):

462 Whole bricks	I House door
114 Half bricks	4 Small windows
70 Angle bricks	4 Large windows
13 I-in. lintels	I Roof No. I
40 2-in. lintels	2 Roofs No. 2
19 3-in. lintels	3 Roofs No. 3
32 Universal pins	

Farm buildings and a farmhouse from a 1941 Minibrix instruction manual (opposite) and 'Brick Cottages, Ministry pattern D15', built for the Ministry of Agriculture and Fisheries at Sutton Bridge, Lincolnshire.

Agricultural prices slumped during the Great Depression and the Ministry sought cheaper materials and cheaper ways of building; for Gunn the answer was simply careful design leading to lower costs. Gunn claimed he learned from his experience that only designs that are easy to build will be cheap.[45] This was always his approach, whether the project was a house[46] or a piggery. It shows in the care he took in designing a pair of piggeries – 'a heavy pig lying against boarding exercises a considerable pressure, which may force off boards that are not put on from the inside' – leading to a design with weatherboard cladding outside and an internal lining of rough elm boards.[47] When it came to houses, Gunn thought good design was not possible unless the architect understood how people were going to use the house. However, he is perhaps best remembered for his design for a dovecote, whereby a drainage vent pipe is disguised by placing a barrel over its top with holes cut out for doves.[48] Sadly the Minibrix Dovecote is not so much fun.

Gunn described himself as 'an ordinary person of solid but strictly limited attainments,'[49] something that architects no longer seem content to be. Among construction toys Minibrix is also solid and worthy, and has limited attainments in the models the average sets could make. With enough money splendid exhibition models were possible, but most Minibrix was used to make small models of ordinary buildings. Whether any of these were designed by the mysterious Mr Carter remains unknown, but much of the built environment was designed by people whose names have been lost. These unknown yet commendable architects believed in what they were doing, often devoting a whole working life to it, and were content to receive a salary in lieu of recognition. They deserve to be remembered.

CHAPTER TEN

Juneero and the
Architecture of
Make-Do-and-Mend

N 1939, AT THE START OF THE SECOND WORLD WAR, a new toy appeared
with timely instructions for building a miniature air-raid shelter from scrap
metal. Juneero is unusual among construction toys in not being a system,
and nor was it cheap. Juneero was a metal workshop in miniature with tools for
pressing, bending, punching and cutting sheet and strip metal. Basically you
could make your own Meccano. The Juneero set came with a supply of material,
but when this ran out scrap metal and old tins could be used. It was a toy for its
time, since the destructive nature of war significantly increases the use of waste
and scrap materials.[1]

However, it seems the German equivalent, Mechanicus, came first. Handles
of the German multi-purpose tool are embossed with 'Mechanicus 1933', something that the later Mechanicus sets of the 1950s and 1960s retained. Mechanicus
comes with instructions for making a basic set of parts that can be assembled into
an exciting wheelbarrow or a lethal-looking pen-and-pencil holder. The postwar
set we have also has a pull-out English translation for making the basic shapes
just in case your German is not up to it.

So British Juneero was arguably a copy of a German toy, like Lott's Bricks
at the end of the First World War. Juneero was also manufactured in the late
1940s in Vancouver.[2] Another British firm soon made its bid for the fingers of
the nation (these are not toys that would pass any modern guidelines for toy

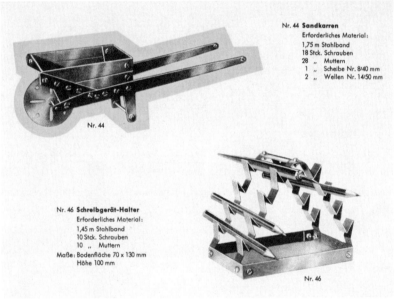

Nr. 44 **Sandkarren**
Erforderliches Material:
1,75 m Stahlband
18 Stck. Schrauben
28 „ Muttern
1 „ Scheibe Nr. 8/40 mm
2 „ Wellen Nr. 14/50 mm

Nr. 44

Nr. 46 **Schreibgerät-Halter**
Erforderliches Material:
1,45 m Stahlband
10 Stck. Schrauben
10 „ Muttern
Maße: Bodenfläche 70 x 130 mm
Höhe 100 mm

Nr. 46

The box lid of a set of Mechanicus c. 1950 (top), and instructions for making a miniature
wheelbarrow and slightly more useful pen and pencil holder.

Boys! this magnificent Signalling Station

JUNEERO
News Letter

Free! design sheets for this model

is but one of the many hundreds of fascinating working models or articles which you can easily make with the new super 1940

JUNEERO

Multi-Purpose TOOL and Materials —the ALL-BRITISH HOBBY

You will get great fun out of making and using this signalling Outfit which will also help you to quickly send and read the famous Morse Code.

Design Sheets Nos. 65 and 66, showing you how to make this Transmitting Station, are given away with the current issue of the Juneero News-letter, price 3d. Order it regularly from your local Juneero dealer.

With a Juneero Set you can actually make real things in metal. PUNCH holes in strips —as many or as few as you like, or BEND them to any angle and in any position.

CUT strips or rods to any length you require. CURVE your strips or rods on the Juneero Scroll tool. There is a CUTTING DIE for cutting threads on the rods—for axles, etc. SHEARS for cutting Juneero metal, glass substitute, etc. Juneero Materials include: METAL SHEETS ruled all ready for you to easily cut to shapes required. CORRUGATED metal for roofs, etc.—very realistic. GLASS SUBSTITUTE for windows, roofs, etc., easily cut to shape or holes punched as desired. GEAR WHEELS, also Pulleys and similar parts for making working models, all ready for you to

DESIGN, MAKE AND FINISH HUNDREDS OF DIFFERENT ARTICLES!

The No. 1 JUNEERO OUTFIT still costs only 12/6. The No. 2 OUTFIT still costs only 25/-. Despite the inclusion of the Super Model Multi-Purpose Tool—prices remain unaltered. You buy JUNEERO OUTFITS from JUNEERO dealers only. If owing to war conditions you have any difficulty, please send your order direct, adding 1/- for carriage and packing, and we will arrange for a set to be sent.

Juneero Ltd., 25, White Street Moorfields, London E.C.2

The 1940 Super Multi-purpose JUNEERO TOOL

A Juneero advertisement from 1940, showing the Juneero multi-purpose tool and the Signalling Station you could produce by using it.

safety) with the issue of Prestacon, also a toy metal press and accessories, in the late 1940s.[3]

Juneero is not really a construction toy like others discussed in this book. It is important because it demonstrates the effort needed to make things from scratch, a situation that many people of the world face when it comes to housing, or indeed anything else that will keep body and soul together. Juneero teaches patience and determination at the same time as imparting fine (and not so fine) motor skills. It is a toy that imitates the architectural experience of make-do-and-mend, and thus relates to that part of the built environment that encompasses shanty towns and the allotment shed. What Juneero demonstrates is the considerable skill needed to make these modest structures out of waste, a skill not shown by some of the other construction toys. Any future where buildings are made with recycled materials may need more skill in the building process than at present. This is because much building is now the assembly of pre-manufactured products rather than construction out of raw materials.

Juneero came with timely instructions for making a toy Anderson air-raid shelter (see below), which included rolling your own corrugated cladding, although you could purchase pre-made cladding as an extra if you had the money. Other instructions extended to making your own Meccano-type metal strips with holes punched for bolts, and there seems not to have been a copyright infringement issue with this do-it-yourself approach. Indeed, Juneero was advertised quite intensively in wartime issues of the *Meccano Magazine*. Not that copyright issues seem to have stopped any of the Meccano imitations, such as Ezy-Bilt or Buz Builder, but at least with Juneero you had the satisfaction of doing it yourself, and the ability to whip up the extra six-hole strip you needed for the model you were trying to construct. There were also instructions for building a blackout lantern and a transmission station, thus emphasizing Juneero's wartime nature.

The real-life Anderson Shelter, designed in 1938 and named after government minister Sir John Anderson, was a corrugated steel hut with a semi-cylindrical roof. It arrived in sections, was sunk about 3 feet (almost a metre) into the ground, covered with earth to a depth of 15 inches (nearly 40 cm)[4] – and could only be used by those with a back garden or yard to put it in. This was unfortunate, for, as the architecture group Tecton had noted in their study of air-raid precautions for the London district of Finsbury, eight out of eleven wards had virtually no yards or gardens of any size.[5] Tecton concluded their 1939 study with the warning that air-raid protection (A.R.P.) needed to be planned to be as efficient as other parts of the country's armaments.[6] When civilian bombing started this advice had not been heeded and the government was criticized, resulting in what might be called 'a tale of two shelters'. After protests about the lack of deep shelters and poor planning for dealing with the turmoil that resulted from air raids in the first month of bombing, Anderson, then Home Secretary, was replaced by the Labour politician Herbert (later Lord) Morrison.[7] His name was given to the Morrison Shelter, introduced in 1941; this was a reinforced-steel dining table the family could shelter under, and didn't need a back garden.

When it came to the two shelters, neither would survive a direct hit from a bomb but were there to protect from the aftermath of bombing, such as flying debris or collapsing walls. *Public Information Leaflet No. 1* (1939) was quite clear on this point, 'Remember that most of the injuries in an air raid are not caused by direct hits by bombs, but by flying fragments of debris or bits of shells.'[8]

Whatever its protective qualities, the curved Anderson Shelter in the back garden,[9] often covered in growing vegetables, was not only an early common example of a building with a green roof, but also became a symbol of doing something at home to outwit the enemy. Somehow, the Morrison shelter, a combined dining table and air-raid shelter, with all the overtones of the equally mismatched Victorian piano-bed,[10] and its cutting-edge engineering,[11] never achieved this level of cult status, even though it seated eight for comfortable, if rather metallic, dining.

In the tale of two shelters, Juneero only made the earlier Anderson; perhaps indicating that, despite its make-do-and-mend approach, a relatively rich uncle was still needed to buy a set. The war-time theme ran through other Juneero instruction leaflets: you can, for example, make a Morse-code transmitter (design sheet 66, price 1d), and a French Tank (design sheet 63, price 1d)[12] – though why not a decent British tank, like the Matilda,[13] remains a mystery. It is even possible to make a rather vestigial Spitfire. You could also make various useful articles around the home, such as a soap dish to hang over the bath (and gently rust) or a rather alarming metal coat hanger that looks set fair to pierce any fabric.[14] There were instructions for a number of farm and railway buildings; these had accessories of printed paper transfers in brick, stone and tile patterns, enabling the buildings to become more permanent and realistic fixtures on model railway layouts.

An Anderson Shelter, reconstructed at the 'Winston Churchill's Britain at War Experience', London.

(Top) A make-do-and-mend building in Jogjakarta, Indonesia, built using materials to hand (brick, corrugated metal, tile, wood, and bamboo), with recycling bins and public transport.

(Above) This accommodation for Chinese workers building a new Eco-city in Tianjin is made from recycled containers – perhaps more eco-friendly than the Eco-city.

However, the fascination of this toy in relation to architecture is not so much that it made buildings, but the fact it was sold as a 'workshop', with the idea that you can make everything yourself, even out of scrap. Juneero, therefore, taught a basic survival mentality as well as engineering. The ethos of Juneero was firmly in the realm of recycling.

At the small scale, the history of building, and hence architecture, is the history of make-do-and-mend building. Buildings, whether to provide shade or keep the rain out, are made from the materials at hand. How they are made reflects the materials available. For many people make-do-and-mend is still the only way they can house themselves and their families, whether the materials are taken directly from the natural environment in the vernacular tradition, or whether they are the waste products of richer societies.

When it comes to architecture, recycling is promoted as a means to achieve sustainable buildings, although the result envisaged is not quite that of the Indonesian example illustrated on the previous page, or even the use of second-hand containers to form a construction workers' village in Tianjin, China. Somehow modern recycling has to meet all the demands of high art, even though most found examples are more happenstance than RIBA-Gold-Medal material.

Architects who wish to be thought of as 'green' often seem to focus on the use of recycled materials as a way of proving their credentials.[15] However, in assessing the overall environmental impact of a building, the biggest benefit to the environment is not to build it. If a building is required, it is much better to re-use an existing building rather than to build a new one, even if the new one is made using recycled materials. And worrying too much about materials is really missing the point anyway, since the energy used to operate the heating, cooling, lighting and equipment is far greater over the building's life than the energy embodied in the materials.[16]

In its instructions for re-using scrap metal, Juneero certainly appears to be a make-do-and-mend toy appropriate to wartime. However, from a slightly different perspective, Juneero could be seen not as a fine example of recycling, but as a part of the consumer society that we all know, love and vote for in the twenty-first century. With Meccano, and with nearly all the other construction sets we have written about, the set comprises a collection of parts that could be assembled to make a model and then taken apart and re-assembled to make a different model. So one day you might make a church and the next day you might take it to pieces and build a library. With Juneero, on the other hand, today's Soap Dish does not become tomorrow's Spitfire; you cannot turn ploughshares into swords with Juneero – or not without enormous difficulty. That wasn't the point of Juneero: the point was to take material – whether new or scrap – and make something permanent. What you have to do is to obtain more resources to build your next model. The Ministry of Fuel and Power understood this connection between objects and resources during the Second World War – '5 lbs of coal saved in one day by 1,500,000 homes will provide enough fuel to build a destroyer. Note: 5 lbs of coal are used in 2 hours by a gas fire or electric oven'.[17] You could have another destroyer but only if you did not have heating or cooking.

You could in principle make your own Meccano with your Juneero tool, but the instructions did not deal with this aspect at all: each sheet of Juneero instructions was for one particular model. This was good business for Juneero as, with luck, you would buy more materials from them to save having to cut up salvaged metal. Prestacon, another multi-purpose tool toy, took the logical next step of making an outfit that would build only one model. The box lid of their No. 66 Outfit shows a double-decker bus, a Jeep, a mobile crane and a large bridge in the background, but the outfit builds only a six-wheeled lorry.[18] The style of the graphics of the Prestacon instructions looks very like that used for the instructions of Castos concrete construction sets,[19] which made toys that could not be taken apart and re-used, and are discussed in the next chapter; one might conjecture that the same minds were behind them both. So these sets that dated from the age of austerity seem to have been driven by a consumerist ideology that runs completely counter to this. *O tempora. O mores.*[20]

CHAPTER ELEVEN

Castos and Concrete on the Carpet

ASTOS WAS A BUILDING set for making miniature reinforced-concrete
buildings, which appeared in 1947.[1] Its rather impressive aim, among
other things, was to put an end to war. This was to be achieved through
providing examples of 'the finest specimens [of architecture] known to ancient
and modern civilizations…'. Castos 'widens understanding of other countries
and helps to destroy the barriers of ignorance which lead to disputes and strife
between the nations.' It certainly looked for an international market. It was
'Patented in Great Britain, the Dominions, U.S.A. and other countries'[2] and by
November 1948 it was advertised in Australia, in *Hobbies Illustrated*.[3] Precisely a
year later it was on special offer in Australia with the price reduced by 23 per
cent,[4] so maybe it was not such a great success in spite of its global ambitions.
The leaflet provided with the set refers to its creation by 'a famous engineer' in
the odd moments when he was not either 'building houses by the thousands for
the League of Nations and other organizations, erecting towers or constructing
bridges…'. Who this engineer was is not divulged and remains a mystery.
Sir Owen Williams seems a good candidate, but he never did any houses.[5]

According to the Australian advertisement, and the pencilled price on the
box of one of the two Castos sets we own, both discovered in New Zealand, the
price of a set was £4 15s 6d. In 1947 this was a lot of money. It would buy you
ninety-five copies of *Hobbies Illustrated* or, also advertised in the magazine, the

Maurlyn Manufacturing Pty Ltd's Silver Chief Aluminium Clockwork Train set (at £3 15s 11d)[6] and leave some change. To give an idea of the present cost, according to the Reserve Bank of New Zealand's Inflation Calculator,[7] £4 15s 6d in the last quarter of 1947 would be worth around NZ$330 in the second quarter of 2011, or more than £175 (US$275) at the current rate of exchange. This was not a cheap toy, but then perhaps putting an end to war is worth paying for.

Architects have long considered concrete to be one of the 'new materials'.[8] However, it is not that new, having been widely used in Ancient Rome. There it replaced quarried stone to build the fast-track buildings that gave the quick results a Roman politician needed to show the people he had achieved something during his eighteen-month term;[9] *plus ça change....* Concrete was certainly used to great effect by the Romans to build, among other things, the dome of the Pantheon[10] – still the world's largest unreinforced concrete dome[11] – and the wall commissioned by the Emperor Hadrian to keep the Scots out of Roman Britain. Given the long history of the material, it is perhaps surprising that there are not more toys based on concrete. It has become ubiquitous not just as a building material but for the modern infrastructure of most urban environments, such as roads, bridges and drainage channels. Concrete is now claimed as the most frequently used material in the construction industry.[12]

The big problem with concrete construction, whether on the carpet or on the building site, is that the shape of the building has to be constructed, the material poured in and allowed to set, and then the outer casing removed later, just like moulding a jelly. Instead of building your wall in just one process, you have to go through three complex and labour-intensive stages. You start by building a life-size hollow wooden model of the proposed dwelling. This is called the 'formwork' (or 'boxing' down under). You then fill your wooden mould with steel reinforcement, to make the concrete stand up. (The Romans made extensive use of unreinforced concrete which has stood up for two thousand years, but that is not the modern way.) You then pour concrete into your steel-filled mould and vibrate it so as to make sure that your concrete is not full of air holes. Finally, once the concrete has cured properly, you remove the mould. And there is your magnificently simple concrete home.

In fact, concrete is a seemingly counter-intuitive substance to use for building; it is the only runny structural material, and it is the only example where you throw away half the materials after you've made the building (even if you have re-usable formwork it still has to be erected and taken apart).

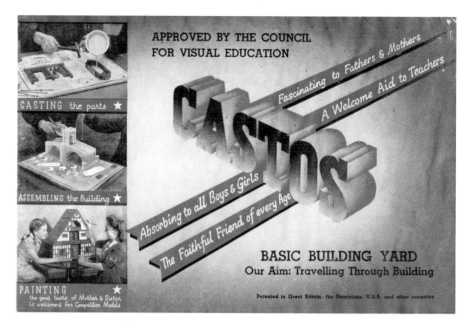

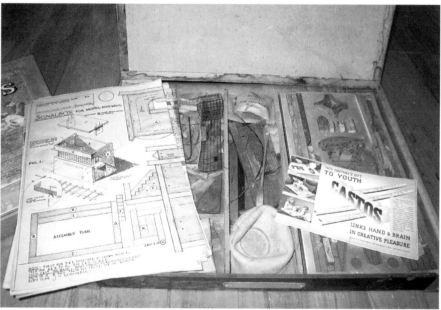

A Castos instruction book (top) and the Castos set with parts and plans for a modern signal box.

Given all its difficulties, it seems very hard to see why you would bother with concrete for many three-dimensional building tasks, but it has had plenty of eager fans. Thomas Edison got caught up in the idea of making a house all in one piece out of concrete, but only so that he could sell cement. At the end of the nineteenth century, when his New Jersey iron ore mine became unprofitable because of the falling price of iron ore, Edison bought a limestone quarry, shipped the redundant ore-crushing machinery to it, and used the crushed limestone to make cement. To sell all this cement he began to experiment with concrete houses, attracting the attention of, among others, Archduke Franz Ferdinand of Austria–Hungary (whose assassination started the First World War), who was keen to build cheap and sanitary houses. (There is always a hope that concrete houses will be proof against vermin, but the clever rats can still get in via the roof – as we know for a fact, since we live in an architect-designed concrete house built in 1939; fortunately the local rat catcher does a good job.) Edison's houses were to be poured in one go and then left to cure for six days before stripping the re-usable moulds to leave a completed house ready for occupants.[13]

Edison attracted the interest of the philanthropist Henry Phipps, who had founded Phipps Houses (still going strong) in 1905 with a million dollars, to provide low-cost housing for the working classes in New York.[14] Edison's low-cost sanitary concrete houses were going to have cast concrete furniture, and even cast concrete pianos and phonographs, and would rent for $7.50 a month, but it all came to nothing. One problem was the start-up costs as the set of moulds alone cost $175,000[15] – a huge amount in today's terms. Some Edison-style concrete houses were indeed built by the watch entrepreneur, Charles Ingersoll, in Union, New Jersey, and they are still there. A contemporary photograph of the houses under construction shows both the scale of the formwork and the sheer mechanical problem of filling a two-storey-high mould with concrete.[16]

This was not a problem faced by 1993's Turner Prize-winner, Rachel Whiteread, who created a concrete memory of a two storey-house in an East London street. Rather than creating walls, Whiteread filled the void created by the envelope of the house with concrete and plaster, thus making the abstract space of what constitutes 'home' into a solid.[17] The council must have had a hard job demolishing it the following year.

One wonders why Edison did not design single-storey houses, which would have been both simpler to build and perhaps more expressive of the American tradition. After all, Buckminster Fuller's 1940s Dymaxion House is a bungalow (see Chapter 5).

Although not the simplest of materials for building a whole house, concrete works really well for horizontal slabs, which can use the ground as one side of the slab, while the top surface can be levelled off with a trowel or its power-operated equivalent. The only formwork you need is around the edges. This may explain why tilt-up slab construction appeared quite early on in the development of reinforced concrete; this is also the way to make a Castos concrete building. With tilt-up slab construction, concrete walls are cast on the ground and then tilted up (hence the name) to form the building. It seems to have been invented by Robert Aiken, a contractor in Illinois early in the twentieth century.[18] One of Aiken's early examples of this technique was the Mess Hall at Camp Perry Military Reservation on the shore of Lake Erie in Ohio. Aiken's tilt-up Mess Hall was damaged by high winds in 1998 and subsequently demolished in 2001, sadly, as it was one of very few remaining early tilt-up structures left in the US. There is a similarity between tilt-up construction and traditional timber building techniques, in which the frames are assembled on the ground and then raised into place. Aiken's early buildings were cast on a bed of sand, before he moved to the use of a flat wooden formwork on steel supports, but still near the ground. The walls for the Mess Hall were tilted up with the use of an engine. In the best traditions of new technology, the building was late, and finally had to be completed by the state in 1909, after the contractor went bankrupt. The final cost was $42,000 rather than the tender price of $16,000.[19] (This phenomenon is known to economists as 'sunk cost theory' – in making decisions on whether it is worth spending money to complete a project, you should discount what's already been spent – or, since the 1970s as the 'Concorde Fallacy';[20] it is also called throwing good money after bad, but not in academic journals.)

Tilt-up slab construction has gone on to be widely used, although it was not until the introduction of mobile cranes in the 1940s that it really got going. Now tilt-up construction is used for over 15% of industrial buildings in the US and, for instance, nearly 75% of commercial buildings in Texas.[21]

Castos is most like tilt-up slab construction in the full-size world. The Castos builder makes moulds by nailing shaped pieces of wood into place flat on the ground (well, on the fibreboard back of the aluminium box lid that is used as the 'working table') to form suitable moulds. The wooden formers, pre-cut into the right shapes for the building plans provided, are supplied with the set.

PAINTING ★
the good taste of Mother & Sister
is welcomed for Competition Models

Setting up the Castos formwork (top) in which the 'concrete' was poured, and Mother helping to paint the finished structure, putatively modelled on one of the Tennessee Valley dams.

No.　　COPYRIGHT CASTOS LT.D *Afoumerfeld*

SERIES 1: *ANCIENT BUILDINGS*
THE BRITISH ISLES
Monk Wearmouth
Church
────DURHAM────

SHEET
1

North Front

West Front

Monk Wearmouth (sic) Church in Castos (above) and St Peter's Church, Monkwearmouth, in stone.

The Castos builder is always referred to as 'he'. Girls are encouraged to play a part in the great Castos project, and certainly when the builder comes to painting his finished model, 'he may have the enthusiastic help of sister or mother.'[22] Having made his moulds, he then adds thin wire reinforcement, pours the 'concrete' (which he mixed from 'Castos building powder' and water) to form the pieces, and then, when they have set, stands them up and pins them to assemble them into a building. The wooden formers could be re-used, but once the supply of reinforcing and/or building powder ran out the set was useless unless further product was bought or substituted. As with full-sized concrete structures, this is doing three lots of building – the formwork, the reinforcement and the casting, but then in Castos there is a fourth stage (as there is with tilt-up construction): that of assembling the precast panels. At least the formwork is re-usable.

Some beautifully clear, whimsically coloured plans came with the Castos set and an acetate sheet was supplied (as was a little rubber mixing bowl to make the concrete in) to be laid over the plans so they were not ruined by the casting process. Castos was not a toy that produced models of buildings made of non-building materials like plastic or rubber; it was a model of the process of making concrete. But it did not stick to making models of concrete buildings. Apart from a church and a bridge, the manufacturers state that a new model will be issued every month, citing the 'Eddystone Lighthouse, the Tennessee Valley Dam, the Tower of London and Donnington Castle' by name, as well as more generic buildings, including 'Railway Stations, Modern Industrial Units' and, bizarrely in reinforced concrete, 'Biblical Architecture.'[23]

Certainly Castos did not shy away from seeking publicity. The back of the instruction book[24] carries endorsements from 'Leading Authorities' comprising a 'Public School Headmaster' who praises it for being 'a boy's introduction to the Muses'; a 'Government Architect' who enthuses how a child will develop his 'appreciation of good proportion' while 'enjoying every minute of the process'; and a 'Museum Curator' who points out how 'reading, making, art, architecture, handiwork and history are all involved.' Two of the three (not the Headmaster) also suggest that adults will not be able to keep their hands off the Castos set. The only named Authority is Sir Charles Reilly OBE. 'the famous British architect' who says, rather chillingly, 'What started as a toy to do something for architecture may, in the end, train a new race of architects to design and build the new world, and create a race of sociologists to conceive for it new and happier and more efficient social relationships.' (Oh brave new world!) Reilly was a

Professor of Architecture at Liverpool University and the first chairman of the RIBA board of architectural education. He became converted to modernism in the late 1930s after a career espousing a more classical approach to design. He was both a charismatic figure and an inspirational teacher who endorsed Castos a year before his death in 1948.[25]

The Castos building plans raise another issue: whether to view concrete as a substitute for other building materials or as a something that could give rise to its own type of architecture. Plans are provided for a model of historic Monk Wearmouth Church (actually, St Peter's, Monkwearmouth) in Tyne and Wear, founded in 665 according to the plans, and of Monnow Bridge in Monmouth dating from 1272. Choosing these ancient structures to be built by tilt-up slab construction is a long way from the modernist view of materials having their own fundamental characteristics that architecture needs to express. Castos did include plans for a perfectly satisfactory modernist concrete signal box that would not look out of place outside Surbiton Station, as well as a concrete foot-bridge and some modernist concrete station canopies, so they followed the line of Bassett-Lowke and Hornby with regard to model railway buildings, although Castos buildings are more suited in scale to O gauge than OO.

In many ways Castos represents the way that concrete is often a hidden material in the construction industry. Although concrete is ubiquitous there are not very many buildings, especially in Britain, that celebrate raw concrete as a substance. Those that do, such as the South Bank Complex and the National Theatre in London, manage to look singularly depressing when it rains. Le Corbusier's *béton brut* (raw concrete) only works in a sunny climate. In Britain the white geometric forms of modernism were usually achieved through using ren-dered brickwork, and they needed a coat of paint at regular intervals to achieve the modern look. The Midland Hotel in Morecambe (mentioned in Chapter 1) is a good example.[26] A few architects in Britain, such as Berthold Lubetkin's prac-tice, Tecton, did make concrete buildings that celebrated concrete, including the iconic Penguin Pool at London Zoo and a house at Gidea Park.[27] This house, which is painted, was showing signs of staining when visited in April 2007, in spite of a recent refurbishment, demonstrating the difficulty of maintaining the pristine appearance that such designs require.

There is nothing formally deterministic about using concrete, as shown in the plans offered with Castos, and in examples from real life. The Tecton house at Gidea Park was built in 1933–34 and features reinforced concrete walls, steel

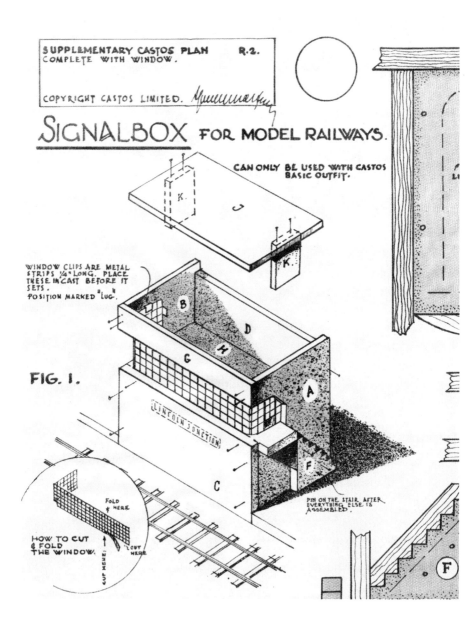

SUPPLEMENTARY CASTOS PLAN   R.2.
COMPLETE WITH WINDOW.

COPYRIGHT CASTOS LIMITED.

SIGNALBOX FOR MODEL RAILWAYS.

CAN ONLY BE USED WITH CASTOS
BASIC OUTFIT.

WINDOW CLIPS ARE METAL
STRIPS ¼" LONG. PLACE
THESE IN CAST BEFORE IT
SETS.
POSITION MARKED "LUG".

FIG. 1.

LINCOLN JUNCTION

FOLD
& HERE

HOW TO CUT
& FOLD
THE WINDOW.

CUT HERE
CUT
HERE

PIN ON THE STAIR AFTER
EVERYTHING ELSE IS
ASSEMBLED.

The Castos Signal Box (opposite) and that at Wimbledon Station, south London, looking slightly worse for wear.

The reinforced concrete house by architects Tecton, built for the 1934 Exhibition at Gidea Park, south London.

windows and a concrete staircase. We live in a small house called Tawa Dell, built in Wellington in 1939 by the New Zealand architect James Walter Chapman-Taylor;[28] it has reinforced concrete walls, steel windows and a concrete staircase. That list of materials and that date imply a modern house in the manner of Tecton, but Tawa Dell, like all Chapman-Taylor's houses, is an Arts and Crafts cottage, with exposed timber beams and doors made of adzed boards. Castos could be seen as entirely rational in its approach, because there is no reason a concrete house has to look modern.

Castos lives on, in spirit at least, in a more modern tilt-up slab model-building system called Linka, first produced in 1979 by the Scottish-based firm of Thomas Salter, and now owned by a US-based company operating as Linka World.[29] Linka uses a series of re-usable rubber moulds to cast accurately textured plaster wall and roof panels that can then be stuck together to make buildings in OO scale (1:76). As with Castos, the buildings you can make with Linka are various: there are brick ones, stone ones, wood-clad ones and even log ones, but there are no examples of concrete modernism. After all, concrete can be made into any shape you want.

CHAPTER TWELVE

Bilt-E-Z, Girder and Panel, Arkitex and the Brave New World

M OST OF THE BUILDING SETS DISCUSSED up to now have been suitable for constructing comfortable low-rise buildings, such as houses, libraries and seaside pavilions. Many sets, Mobaco and Bayko, for example, specifically excluded tall buildings by not providing long-enough posts or rods for supporting such grand designs. Although stacking bricks and blocks of all shapes and sizes have always been used to make towers – and part of their fun is to see how high you can build before the lot collapses – it was the US, home of the skyscraper, that provided the first construction toys for making high buildings. Bilt-E-Z appeared in the 1920s and made very good imitation stepped-back tall buildings, like those then appearing along the streets of New York and Chicago. Later toys followed, with Girder and Panel and the British Arkitex making realistic modern skyscrapers.

Tall buildings have been an object of desire since ancient times. The Great Pyramid at Giza was originally about 146 metres (480 ft) high[1] and the story of the Tower of Babel is a good example of the hubris that comes with building tall.[2] The key message is that God thought that if the people got the Tower of Babel built, they would be able to do anything, so He put a stop to excessive techno-logical development, which might create a rival centre of power. Hardly surprising, therefore, that building a tower is a way for architects and engineers to put their mark on the world – towers are just so gloriously visible.

The Bilt-E-Z instruction manual, showing the type of buildings that could be made (top); they resemble the 1914 Michigan Central Station in Detroit, designed by hotel architects Warren and Wetmore and closed by Amtrak in 1988.

The Tower of Babel was a brick structure, made of good strong fired bricks. Bricks have been popular for the construction of towers for millennia. In 1049, during the Song Dynasty of China, the Iron Pagoda in Kaifeng, Henan Province was built to replace a wooden pagoda that was destroyed by lightning.[3] It is not actually made of iron but of fireproof brick, which takes on the colour of iron when seen at a distance, and has withstood many earthquakes as well as the flooding of the nearby Yellow River. The pagoda is 57 metres (187 ft) tall. Europe's tall buildings were also religious, but usually made of stone. The stone towers of Lincoln Cathedral (completed around 1280) now stand 83 metres (270 ft) high, but originally there was a lead-clad wooden spire, which was reputed to make it the tallest building in the world, overtopping the Great Pyramid of Giza, until the spire blew down in a storm in 1549.[4]

In the nineteenth century, when capitalism really got into its stride, there was new pressure to build high, not to the glory of Buddha or God, but for commercial profit. This development took place largely in the United States, particularly in Chicago and New York. Brick reached its apotheosis in the 16-storey Monadnock Building in Chicago designed by Burnham and Root in 1891. This was a loadbearing brick office building 66 metres (215 ft) high, taller than the Iron Pagoda. At ground level the walls were 1.8 metres (6 ft) thick, tapering to 0.46 metres (1½ ft) at the top,[5] and we were told as architecture students that the building was as tall as it could get before the extra space added at the top was lost at the bottom, where the ground floor walls would have to be made thicker to carry the extra load. A four-block complex eventually comprised the Monadnock, Kearsage, Katahdin and Wachusett buildings (all named after mountains in New England); the Wachusett Building, completed in 1893, was designed by Holabird and Roche following the early death of John Root. Rather than using brickwork to carry the building's load, they used a steel frame clad with a non-loadbearing wall – a curtain wall – of brick and terracotta. This proved a significantly cheaper method of construction, and set the pattern for subsequent skyscraper development

The (rubber) brick skyscraper plan offered to the owner of the largest Minibrix set does therefore reflect a real precedent, in terms of brick towers, but one that died out in the real world before the end of the nineteenth century. From this point on, it was the steel frame that made the tall building possible. The use of steel is well reflected in the first popular skyscraper building set, called Bilt-E-Z, which is, unsurprisingly, American. (If British, the name would be pronounced 'Built Ee Zed'.) Bilt-E-Z was produced in the 1920s by the Scott Manufacturing Company, Inc. based in Chicago,[6] the ancestral home of the skyscraper. A 1927 advertisement in the *Pittsburgh Press*[7] says that the set 'Builds tunnels, train sheds, bridges, etc., for your train set – skyscrapers, garages, movie houses, in fact, practically every structure real architects build.' And the advert adds, 'All materials chemically treated to make them sanitary', just like Bayko, which could be boiled to kill germs, although in the case of Bilt-E-Z the chemical treatment was just paint. Right from the start the box lid, which was originally a monochrome image and later appeared in colour, shows both a boy and a girl enjoying some building together, although it is subtitled 'the boy builder', and inside the book of instructions, as well as 'The ideal toy for girl or boy' it states rather more emphatically 'As the boy builds the toy the toy builds the boy.'[8] The National Museum of Building in Washington, D.C. has several examples of Bilt-E-Z in its Architectural Toy Collection, which was originally assembled over 30 years by George Wetzel from Chicago.[9]

The bridges between buildings shown on the Bilt-E-Z plans and box lid never became as common in real life as early science fiction illustrators – with their dreams of towers and aerial walkways – had hoped.[10] However, real American buildings of the era, such as the now abandoned Michigan Central Station in Detroit, do definitely look as if they have been constructed out of Bilt-E-Z.

Bilt-E-Z makes great models of tall buildings but it does not reflect their process of construction. The models have loadbearing steel walls just like Wenebrik, but whereas Wenebrik panels pretended to be loadbearing bricks, the various Bilt-E-Z wall components are storey-height panels. These have flanges at top and bottom, and slot into square steel floor panels, which are connected together by separate flat steel plates to form the floor slab. These floor/roof panels are formed from two thin steel sheets ingeniously interconnected so that they have a full-width slot on all four sides, into which the flanges of the walls can slide. You then add shaped steel cornices to provide a neat finish at the top. You also have to add internal walls to hold it all up if your planned building is more than a couple of bays thick. Bilt-E-Z was remarkably versatile, it came in a range of colours, and it also allowed the construction of setbacks and stepped buildings and, as noted above, bridges to connect together two towers. This is in spite of having relatively few different components, and is a function of its inherent lack of constructional realism. What you build with Bilt-E-Z is a curtain-wall

A British Chad Valley Girder and Panel Set (above and opposite) showing a complete modern city, but note the American trains, the fire engine, the Greyhound bus and the American flags, making it seem very un-British.

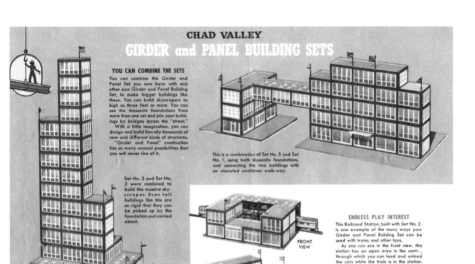

CHAD VALLEY
GIRDER and PANEL BUILDING SETS

YOU CAN COMBINE THE SETS

You can combine the Girder and Panel Set you now have with any other size Girder and Panel Building Set, to make bigger buildings like these. You can build skyscrapers as high as three feet or more. You can use the Masonite foundations from more than one set and join your buildings by bridges across the "street."

With a little imagination, you can design and build literally thousands of new and different kinds of structures. "Girder and Panel" construction has so many unusual possibilities that you will never tire of it.

This is a combination of Set No. 3 and Set No. 1, using both Masonite foundations, and connecting the two buildings with an elevated cantilever walk-way.

Set No. 3 and Set No. 2 were combined to build this massive skyscraper. Even tall buildings like this are so rigid that they can be picked up by the foundation and carried about.

ENDLESS PLAY INTEREST

This Railroad Station, built with Set No. 2, is one example of the many ways your Girder and Panel Building Set can be used with trains and other toys.

As you can see in the *front* view, this station has an open area in the centre, through which you can load and unload the cars while the train is in the station.

This is only one of many types of railroad stations, bus stations, air terminals, garages, fire houses, etc. that you can build.

FRONT VIEW

BACK VIEW

MODERN CANTILEVER CONSTRUCTION—*Possible Only With* GIRDER and PANEL BUILDING SETS

Because of the "triangle bracing" principle which gives such rigidity to buildings constructed with these sets, it is possible to use modern effects such as overhanging upper stories, as in the building at the left.

BE A CONSTRUCTION ENGINEER

When you have become familiar with the many ways to use your Girder and Panel Building Set, you can design and construct engineering projects like the elevated trestle at the right. These are the only all-plastic building sets that let you build with girders like structural steel, with prefabricated panels for walls and roofs.

construction in which the 'curtain wall' is loadbearing – a complete contradiction. In this sense Bilt-E-Z is very like Bayko, in that its construction technology is not in any way related to the buildings that it produces.

It was not until 1956 that a toy appeared that imitated the construction of modern tall buildings, with a frame and cladding. The manufacturer was the Peter-Austin Manufacturing Co. of Toronto, Canada. They made two different sets, the No. 500 Trans-Canada Highway Bridge set and the No. 510 Building Set. These sets comprised columns and girders made of rigid red polystyrene.[11] The columns were pushed into a baseboard of Masonite (hardboard) with holes to receive them, and they were then connected with the horizontal girders to form a building frame of any desired height, which could then be clad with lightweight panels of thin, vacuum-formed plastic, incorporating combinations of glazing and opaque walls. Like Bilt-E-Z, the simplicity of the system allows for a variety of building forms. A year later, in 1957, Kenner Products of Cincinnati, Ohio produced a more or less exact copy of the Canadian sets under the names of 'Girder and Panel' and 'Bridge and Turnpike' in what appears to be a commercial rip-off. Certainly pictures of both systems show remarkable similarities. As might be expected, the Wikipedia entry for Girder and Panel does not have the full story.[12] It describes how it was invented by the president of Kenner, Albert Steiner, after he saw a new building being constructed in Cincinnati, but this appears to be contradicted by the pictures of the Canadian sets, which predate the Kenner product.[13]

The toy industry has a history of the original inventor not being the one who made a success of the idea, as happened with the Lilienthals and Richter's Blocks. Whatever the truth of who got there first, it was Kenner who made a go of frame construction for building toys, and the sets were very successful, particularly once the rather brittle polystyrene girders were replaced by more flexible high-density polyethylene. They were also made under licence in the UK, starting in 1958, by the Chad Valley company in Birmingham, who made all kinds of toys, from teddy bears to train sets. The only difference is that the Bridge and Turnpike sets became Bridge and Roadway sets, although it still features American trains on the bridges, and the cars and lorries drive on the right.

The original Girder and Panel sets, both Canadian and American, were of a scale that fitted with the O gauge model trains that were the American norm; these were made by firms including Lionel[14] (still making trains in 2012[15]), American Flyer,[16] and, for the poorer boys, Marx.[17] On the 'Girder and Panel and

Bridge and Turnpike Heaven' website there are photographs of a magnificent cityscape, with both O gauge trains and streetcars (trams), incorporating many Girder and Panel buildings and showing the variety possible with these sets.[18] The night-time pictures are particularly convincing.

By the late 1950s, however, O gauge trains had almost disappeared from the UK market. Even Hornby were winding down their clockwork system. So a toy that made O gauge buildings was not likely to find a great market. Into this breach stepped Tri-ang, makers of OO gauge trains, with a system called Arkitex, introduced in 1959.[19] This was similar to Girder and Panel in concept, being a frame which was then clad, but it had two principal differences. The first was that it was made in two parallel versions so it tied in with other Tri-ang products, namely Tri-ang Railways (OO scale or 1:76) and Spot-On diecast cars (1:42). Both of these were introduced as direct competition for the well known Meccano products, Hornby Dublo trains and diecast Dinky Toy vehicles.

The second difference between Arkitex and its American original, other than scale, was that Arkitex was made of rigid materials, rather than the somewhat bendy girders and thin flexible claddings of Girder and Panel. In spite of this, at OO scale it is extremely hard to make the components sit exactly square with each other. As a consequence, Arkitex buildings can often look as if they have been through a minor earthquake or suffered blast damage. There are some good photographs of this phenomenon in the Arkitex section of the very comprehensive Tri-ang Railways website, showing some large Arkitex buildings built by James Day.[20]

The rigidity of Arkitex made for very realistic models, but at the same time it also acted as a powerful determinant of form. This is mirrored by steel-frame construction in real life. Architects from Louis Sullivan to I. M. Pei who have embraced the vocabulary of the steel frame with cladding seem to have come to the same conclusion: often all you can do is to give the same old tower a different treatment at top and bottom.

Arkitex had another limitation. The vacuum-formed cladding panels of Girder and Panel came in a variety of types and shapes, because they were fairly easy to produce, whereas the injection-moulded glazing panels of Arkitex offered only one change: the slot-in steel spandrel panels under the glazing were blue on one side and red on the other, so your building could be all red, all blue, or an exciting combination of the two for the budding Mondrian, all in a white frame. In later sets, the panels foreshadowed the postmodern colour palette with

Arkitex Set B, with which you can only construct a box-shaped building (above), but even this is making the young architect concentrate hard; an Arkitex-style building in Geneva (opposite), at least follows the form and scale of the older buildings in the street, but needs a lot more heating because of all that glass.

panels of pastel green and blue.[21] There were also solid cladding panels, originally in white and later in brick colour, but again design opportunities were limited to where you put them.

If you could not afford the bigger sets even marginally more exciting buildings with stepped façades or overhangs were out of reach, as the smaller sets allowed only rigid cubic forms. You could build a tall thin block or a low wide one, but that was about it.

This limitation on what you can build is highly realistic. Arkitex, and to a slightly lesser extent Girder and Panel, both demonstrate the fundamental problem of prefabrication, which is that you need a lot of different parts if you want to make anything more complicated than a simple box. Having to have a large range of different parts then destroys the theoretical advantage of prefabrication, which is the factory mass production of the building bits. If you need too many different parts they become one-offs and you are back to building by hand.

A telling thing is the inclusion of signboards in all these sets, so that you can tell what the generic buildings are supposed to be. In the early American Girder and Panel sets, the signs say things like Drug Store; WUSA-TV; City Motel; and 5¢ and 10¢ Store. In the English version of Girder and Panel they include Bus Terminus; J. Stone, Estate Agent; Sweetshop and Milk Bar; Palace Hotel; Acme Toy Co.; Telephone Exchange; T.V. Studio; and, in Arkitex very specifically, F. W. Woolworth & Co. Ltd, MacFisheries Food Centre, J. Sainsbury, Marks & Spencer, and Burton Tailoring.[22] Without the names the buildings are all the same.

One advantage of Arkitex and Girder and Panel was that, because they imitated the process of construction, they did make buildings that looked convincing even when unfinished, something of which you could not accuse Bayko or Wenebrik. This meant that you could use the sets to make realistic models of construction sites as well as finished buildings. [23]

Tri-ang's Arkitex came on the market in 1959, and made accurate models of the sort of buildings that were being constructed all over the world. In Britain they appeared in the New Towns as well as in the traditional city centres that were being so enthusiastically destroyed by the drive to modernize. Both Arkitex and Girder and Panel built rectilinear blocks, an architectural form that has become almost universal in modern urban contexts. This was noted by the architectural and design writer Jonathan Glancey: '...I adored Arkitex, a scale model

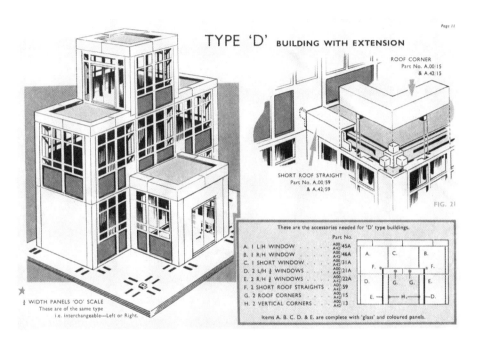

TYPE 'D' BUILDING WITH EXTENSION

ROOF CORNER
Part No. A.00/15
& A.42/15

SHORT ROOF STRAIGHT
Part No. A.00/59
& A.42/59

FIG. 21

¾ WIDTH PANELS 'OO' SCALE
These are of the same type
i.e. Interchangeable—Left or Right.

These are the accessories needed for 'D' type buildings.

		Part No.
A.	1 L/H WINDOW	A00/45A A42/
B.	1 R/H WINDOW	A00/46A A42/
C.	1 SHORT WINDOW	A00/31A A42/
D.	2 L/H ¾ WINDOWS	A00/21A A42/
E.	2 R/H ¾ WINDOWS	A00/22A A42/
F.	2 SHORT ROOF STRAIGHTS	A00/59 A42/
G.	2 ROOF CORNERS	A00/15 A42/
H.	2 VERTICAL CORNERS	A00/13 A42/

Items A. B. C. D. & E. are complete with 'glass' and coloured panels.

Exciting options for moving beyond the box (at least to an aggregation of boxes) were offered by Arkitex Set C.

(Top) An Arkitex tower under construction still looks quite convincing.

(Above) An undeniably Arkitex-style building project in the Chaoyang District of Beijing, the Jianwai Soho Apartments in 2007; an office and residential development, it was designed by architect Riken Yamamoto.

construction set made by Tri-ang with which I could build glum modern office blocks to stand alongside my OO-scale railway.'[24] These sets, and Girder and Panel, which also made excellent high-rise blocks, allowed the construction of a whole urban infrastructure, offering, in Girder and Panel's case, not the steam locomotives, diesel railcars and red buses of Tri-ang, but working monorails. This was the brave new world to come that has now come, and become all too familiar.

Girder and Panel and Arkitex originated in the 1950s and made models of the buildings of that time, but these buildings are still being constructed today, largely because this is still a profitable way to build.

CHAPTER THIRTEEN

▨ Playplax
▨
▨ and
▨
▨ Deconstruction

P
LAYPLAX AND DECONSTRUCTION may both seem odd topics to include in
a book about construction toys and architecture. Playplax is not really
a construction toy since it does not set out to make identifiable buildings
or engineering structures. It even comes without instructions. Deconstruction –
also known as deconstructivism – is about challenging conventional notions of
architecture. It is an odd term to apply to architecture, unless you happen to
be in the demolition and materials recovery business, but it is allied to the
philosophical movement called deconstruction, in what is now seen as an
analogous, rather than a direct, way. This movement arose from philosopher
Jacques Derrida's critique of writing as a method for the transmission of truths
(holding that there are no truths, just interpretations), although architecture is,
in essence, to do with making things, not words or signs.

Playplax is here because we have always loved it. The toy was invented by
designer Patrick Rylands in 1966.[1] It consisted of a single component, polystyrene squares 2 x 2 inches (5 x 5 cm) with a ½-inch (13-mm) slot in the centre of
each side, so the pieces can be slotted together to make three-dimensional
objects. The pieces were translucent, and were red, green, blue, yellow or clear.
First made in 1967 by Trendon, a plastics moulding company that built up a toy
business,[2] the boxed sets were soon embellished with stickers from the Design
Centre, the British promoter of good taste in commercial design; Playplax won a

Design Centre award in its first year,[3] and in the first three years of manufacture over a million sets were sold, with exports to thirty countries.[4] This is hardly surprising, as the toy just makes beautiful things. Whatever you do, the result is pretty stunning, so it is no surprise that it finished up as part of the permanent collection of the New York Museum of Modern Art.[5]

In 1968 cylinders (called 'rings') were added to the range, but somehow these have never appealed to us; packing them into the box again does not give the same satisfaction as arranging the squares and deciding how to stack the colours. In addition, the Playplax rings already enclose space, whereas the beauty of the squares is that they have to be put together to do so and create a particular space. Trendon packaged the rings and squares together,[6] and made boxes of just rings. For purists (like us) they also made small heavy boxes of 24 Playplax squares, which is how we originally bought the toy when we were students.

There is something delightful in having a small box that is also heavy. Each box contained a single colour and, for some reason we cannot now remember, we bought two boxes of the clear, possibly reflecting the fact that the bigger sets contained more clear squares than coloured. These smaller boxes, with their more abstract design and inscription 'The Creative Construction Set', may have been sold as an educational toy for nurseries and schools, as it is clear from reading Playplax blogs that people played with the toy at school, not just at home on the carpet.

The marketing of Playplax was soon taken over by the much older firm of educational suppliers, James Galt and Co. Galt had established themselves as sellers of toys in 1961 with their pioneering toy shop in Carnaby Street[7] in London (before this location became 'swinging'). Their blue-lidded Playplax box suggested that anyone aged five or over could 'Build creatively in many dimensions with this colourful set of interlocking rings and plates.'[8] The very idea of building implies three dimensions, as there cannot be fewer than that in a structure that is going to contain some kind of human usage, even if only storage of stuff. You might lay the squares out in two-dimensional patterns, but not the rings, and making patterns is more akin to decoration than building. So to arrive at 'many dimensions' you have to move on to at least the fourth and fifth, and preferably more when making anything with Playplax. Time as the fourth seems credible ('You can have another ten minutes and then you have to pack up and go to bed …') but thinking about a fifth dimension lands you well into Einstein's general theory of relativity and more recent string theory,[9] which was probably

A Playplax box of rings (top) and a box of Playpax squares with the Design Centre approval sticker.

not what Patrick Rylands had in mind when he developed the toy in the first place. Still, if string theory is right we all live, and play, in many dimensions, even if the human body restricts what we can feel to three plus time, so maybe the Galt box lid is right after all.

Packaging aside, the delight of Playplax is the way you slot together flat squares to enclose space instantly, with the added pleasure of viewing the light through the filters of different colours, even (with enough layers) to the extent of creating a virtual black. Thus, as any Playplax model is turned and re-examined, what we see changes because it is viewed differently, even though the object remains unchanged. This is the fascination of the toy that probably led to its success. Although production of Playplax ceased in the early 1980s,[10] the toy came back on the market in 2010, though now only the squares are produced. The Stockport factory that made the original Playplax is making the modern version, using the same dye recipes for the colours as before.[11]

There is one problem with Playplax structures. To allow the pieces to slot together and be taken apart there has to be a tolerance – a certain amount of 'give' at the slots. A very satisfactory basic unit can be constructed by interlocking eight pieces together to create a central cubic space with projecting planes. At this stage what can be built has more connection with early modernism's emphasis on abstraction, or even with De Stijl, given the projecting planes that can be continued in each direction (see Mobaco and De Stijl, Chapter 7) than with the disconnected and fragmented buildings that have been linked to deconstruction. However, clearly the next step with Playplax is to continue upwards and so make the ultimate 'glass' tower with its overlapping and interacting transparent colours; this again evokes modernist echoes, such as the glass architecture of Bruno Taut.[12] Since any box of bricks provides the challenge to build upward, making a Playplax tower is an obvious thing to do. It is also disappointing, as the tolerance in the joints means the tower has a (literally) built-in tendency to lean, with the lean increasing as the tower climbs until eventually it topples (at a height of ten pieces). Suddenly all its cubist perfection looks decidedly shaky.

In Playplax, the notion of what a tower should be (vertical, aspiring, rigid) is challenged by the process of construction; this links it to deconstruction. The 1988 catalogue that accompanied the first 'Deconstructivist Architecture' exhibition at the Museum of Modern Art in New York is a good starting-point for understanding deconstruction. In it the architect and academic Mark Wigley stated that deconstruction was powerful because it challenged the basic architectural values of 'harmony, unity, and stability', noting that these are unachievable and that there are always flaws.[13] Deconstructivist architecture just set out to make these flaws apparent. Harmony and unity are arguably in the mind of the observer, but most buildings do actually provide stability, because they stand up, but if an architectural theorist says there are flaws then of course it must be so. This is a different approach to that of the Ancient Greeks, who recognized the inherent visual flaw in the perfectly straight (architecturally un-flawed) column, and through the use of entasis (a slight swelling at the midpoint) endeavoured to make the column appear straight from a distance. Wigley also stated that the point of deconstructivist architecture is to challenge conventional thinking about form.

Playplax would seem to fit this idea perfectly; inherent in its structural properties is a 'flaw' that challenges the very notion of what a building should be – orthogonal, stable, and somehow indicative of the investment in terms of resources and time that have gone into it – leaving in its place something that is not as satisfying as it should be. As one reviewer states, in some ways creating Playplax models works better when you make them flat on the table rather than soaring in three dimensions.[14] Galt's claim of working in many dimensions works best for imaginary structures.

The more elegant link between Playplax and deconstruction is the fact that the sets come without instructions – it is hard to make realistic structures or models of things. Thus the meaning of what the model represents has to be assigned by the child, and children are very good at this. The idea of being able to read meanings into things also provides a link with the philosophical ideas behind deconstruction.

The first major architectural work associated with the deconstruction move-ment is Parc de la Villette, in Paris, designed by Bernard Tschumi with its 'folies'.[15] A folie is essentially a structure with no purpose, but to which meaning can be assigned. This urban park is meant to stand alone, ignoring all precedent urban parks, as a place where the user can explore space and object without prior guidance. But this thought can be challenged by the use of the term 'folie' for the small architectural structures that mark the grid of space within the Parisian park. We can think of Paris, we can think of Manet,[16] think of the Folies-Bergère (Shepherdesses' Follies), think of Marie-Antoinette playing at being a shepherd-ess...and it is then a small step to the urbanization of the countryside and the traditional city park. So, if nothing else, Parc de la Villette could be seen as part of the process of taming and containing the life of the countryside, so that just the right amount of greenery is exhibited and enjoyed within the urban milieu. So, as Derrida has implied of texts, it all depends on how you read it: deconstruction says there is essentially no 'truth' we can all recognize, although even deconstructivist architecture has to conform to the laws of gravity and physics. (There is even contention over how deconstruction should be labelled, let alone what it is: 'Deconstructivist Architecture' was the name of the Museum of Modern Art exhibition discussed above, but deconstruction is the term normally applied to architecture.) The Parc de la Villette can be viewed as something revolutionary, a precursor of a new movement in architecture, or as a different interpretation of the same thing. In the end it is the confusion that is interesting. Tschumi designed a park in 1985 and invited Derrida to be involved;[17] the rest, as they say, is history.

Deconstruction challenges expectations, and the simple truth is that in architecture, whatever the philosophy, doing what looks totally different from what your neighbour has done is a great way to get noticed. An early and famous example of this approach was the 1987 Hysolar Institute building for the University of Stuttgart, by Behnisch and Partners. This was a centre for exploring the making of hydrogen by solar power. Despite the use of prefabricated laboratory components in the construction, it certainly challenges any expectation of what a building for photovoltaic research might be. After all, PV panels do tend to face the sun, and hence have an ordered direction, and they are usually rectangular, but the Hysolar building is nothing if not wonky – elements look skewed and jumbled. Having stood empty for a while, the building has since been renovated and extended and now houses the Institute for Visualisation and Interactive Systems.[18] This makes it seem that what the building is has prompted an appropriate use, and suddenly it looks a whole lot less challenging as architecture. This in itself is suggestive of the human need for order in the face of disorder. Although Derrida may have said there can never be truth (and is that true, we might ask?) it does not stop anyone wanting truth and searching for it. Maybe an architecture of disorder simply seeks to rectify itself over the life of the building by attracting appropriately less ordered activities, or maybe we just get used to it.

In fact the whole approach of deconstruction seems much less radical when we look at another deconstructivist building. We are invited to interpret the three elements that go to make up the Imperial War Museum North in

The 1987 Hysolar Building, Stuttgart, by Behnisch and Partners has now become an Institute for Visualisation and Interactive Systems.

The Imperial War Museum North in Manchester, UK, designed by Daniel Libeskind in 2002.

Manchester as representing the three arenas of war – earth, air and water.[19] Splitting warfare into the operational spheres of Army, Air Force and Navy avoids dealing with biological warfare, propaganda, munitions work, codebreaking or even life on the home front, all of which have played a major part in the history of human warfare. How can a building be part of the ethos of challenge and uncertainty and yet ask to be interpreted in such a simplistic way? Designed by Daniel Libeskind in 2002, the uncomfortable angles and juxtapositions of this building are apparently symbolic of the upheaval of war and are therefore, in that context, not unexpected; it is as if deconstructivism itself had somehow become a suitable – almost conventional – response.

The Hysolar Building is still explicit in how it is put together: that is, we know how the parts are made to fit together even if it looks as if the contractor had been at the magic mushrooms. The Libeskind building, on the other hand, is reticent in how it is constructed, in that the skin and the way the skin makes forms appear – the exterior appearance of the structure – is more important than how the skin is held up. This is obvious in the taller viewing tower – the air arena – which is empty, apart from a viewing platform, and held up inside by a lot of tubular triangulated structure.[20] The emptiness brings to mind the unfortunate suggestion that the effort of aerial warfare was an empty gesture. It probably didn't feel that way to anyone trying to take shelter during a bombing raid.

In other places creating a disjointed building has produced some challenging, not to say uncomfortable, results. The CCTV building in Beijing designed by Rem Koolhaas and built in 2008 to coincide with the Beijing Olympics, is a structure that, as anyone who has played with building bricks would tell you, looks as if it is about to fall down. In fact it is held in this seemingly precarious position by a whole lot of steel; thus what you see is not what you get. It looks unstable but isn't, which also tells you, from experience, that it must have got a lot of something in it in terms of structure, since it patently has not fallen down (yet), in spite of a very serious fire in the adjacent tower in 2009.[21]

So some of the underlying ideas behind deconstruction are still around, even if the buildings related with it have in some way become more 'normal'. The simple fact is that deconstructivist buildings have become familiar and it is harder to find ideas and forms that challenge what architecture is, or could be. At the same time the unusual sells, so, in a consumerist society, what began as a philosophical enquiry has become a neat way to make money. As the architect and academic Neil Leach has commented, capitalism now guides cultural

The somewhat improbable CCTV Building in Beijing, by Rem Koolhaas.

Reflections – a new residential development in Singapore in the wonky style that echoes tall Playplax structures.

production, and this includes architecture.[22] If it looks difficult to build – in other words, wonky – it will probably sell and may even become a tourist attraction; after all it worked for the bell tower at Pisa. It is interesting, not to say ironic, that most of these radical, challenging buildings are monuments to the wealth and capitalism that form the real institutional authority. This authority is challenged far more by South American shanty towns or squatter settlements than by the glossy, if crazy-looking, towers and museums of deconstruction's wealthy practitioners.

However, apart from the contorted and unsettling buildings that have followed on from the deconstructivist approach in architecture, deconstruction is also a way of seeing. It gives a structure the potential to be interpreted in different ways – and this is also the beauty of Playplax. The toy makes lovely abstract objects that, especially because Playplax comes without instructions, require imagination to turn them into structures with a name, such as a house, tower, or hotel.[23] Perhaps more usefully, there are other parallels between deconstruction and Playplax. Deconstruction is not of itself a theory of architecture, but it does question the conventional forms that we think go to make up buildings, and PlayPlax is not a building toy but one that deals in elements (space and boundary) that go to make up buildings. PlayPlax makes clear how architecture is produced, in that it transforms what was nothing into something through the interplay of its transparent and overlapping planes. What Playplax does is create space that not only has no purpose but whose boundaries seem almost suggested rather than defined. Nevertheless, a child building a Playplax structure will have no difficulty in 'naming' a function for it that it patently could not contain. The need to give abstract or nonrepresentational structures a purpose is the basis of so much play. The cardboard box that becomes in turn a house, a car, a ship, or the mud structure that is at one moment a fort and the next a cake for Teddy, are situations that are so familiar and form the basis for so much creativity. Playplax, by not imposing interpretations of structure, channels that creativity in a flexible way.

The philosophy of deconstruction, too, allows many interpretations, but, for us, Playplax is more fun.

CHAPTER FOURTEEN

▦ Lego
▦ and the
▦ Green City

O
F ALL THE CONSTRUCTION TOYS DESCRIBED IN THIS BOOK, Lego is
probably the best known. There cannot be many middle-class parents
over the last fifty years who do not know what it feels like to step with
bare feet onto an unexpected Lego brick lying in wait on the carpet. Lego is a toy
with a long history. The first Lego plastic bricks appeared in 1947, the current
version in 1958, and in 2000 Lego was named 'Toy of the Century' by *Fortune*
magazine in the US and by the Toy Retailers Association in Britain.[1]

The origins of Lego are quite complicated. The basis of Lego, in the beginning, is the interlocking brick. There were interlocking bricks in the 1930s, such
as Bild-O-Brik in the US in 1934[2] and the British Minibrix, which we have
written about in Chapter 9. These bricks offered a limited range of shapes, and
had studs on the bottom that interlocked with corresponding holes in the row of
bricks below. Because they are rubber, the studs on the bricks deform slightly to
lock the bricks securely together.

Next on the scene were the wooden American Bricks, made by Halsam,
makers of the Lincoln Logs that appeared in Chapter 6 (Halsam also made the
earlier, non-studded American Brick Blocks).[3] Halsam was founded in 1917 by
two brothers-in-law, Harold Elliot and Sam Goss, Jr., who combined their names
to form the company's. One source says that Harold's son, Kip, came back from
England, where he had spent time as a child in the 1940s and discovered his

favourite toy, Minibrix; he helped launch American Bricks, which were made using the machinery that Halsam used to mass-produce checkers (draughts to the British) and dominoes.[4] However, another states that the first American Bricks patent was filed in 1939,[5] so the origin is clearly disputed. Perhaps Kip's sojourn in England was in the 1930s rather than during the Blitz; then the whole thing would make sense, as the American Bricks patent is clearly later than that for Minibrix. The basic wooden American Brick has eight raised studs on the top, whereas the basic Minibrix brick has two studs on the bottom, but unlike their rubber predecessors, American Bricks interlock fairly loosely. This means they are fixed in relation to one another and cannot slide around, but they do not stay together if you pick them up. This makes them a halfway house between the plain blocks of Richter's and Lott's and the fully interlocking blocks of Minibrix and Lego.

In some ways American Bricks were a 'green' product. Apparently Sam Goss used to let the workers go home early on days when the factory got too hot,[6] which would mark him as a green employer, or maybe they just didn't have air conditioning; these days the lack of air conditioning might class the factory as a green building. And of course Sam's bricks were made of wood, a natural renewable resource, just like Minibrix, which were made of natural rubber. However, the world was moving away from natural renewable resources towards plastics made from oil (and natural gas).[7] Halsam duly followed the trend, making plastic bricks called, with glorious logic, American Plastic Bricks, which were a close copy of American (wooden) Bricks.[8] Both the wooden and plastic versions had cardboard windows and doors,[9] tastefully printed with curtains and blinds,[10] which fitted into slots in the bricks in the same manner as the celluloid windows of Minibrix. Later the windows changed to plastic ones that could be opened. The roofs are also like Minibrix roofs, but in cardboard rather than rubber, and American Plastic Bricks had lintels, like the Minibrix ones, for spanning openings.[11] When Messrs Elliot and Goss went into plastics moulding in a big way they formed a separate company called Elgo (from Elliot and Goss),[12] which seems to have taken over the manufacture of American Plastic Bricks, although the Elgo sets do not appear to have had lintels.[13] The Australian copy of American Plastic Bricks, called Bilda-Brix, did not have lintels either, but did have narrow metal strips to support the bricks over the openings. These were unconvincingly replaced by bits of cardboard in the New Zealand version of Bilda-Brix.[14] Our experience is that Bilda-Brix definitely do not interlock sufficiently to allow a

INGENIOUS

American Bricks

Here are play hours full of intriguing and educational fun. Sets range from 58 to over 200 pieces.
Many families buy set after set of LOGS and BRICKS—permanent models —houses, bridges, etc.—are built at small expense — eventually complete frontier towns and modern cities result.

CA'S OLDEST

An early interlocking Lego-style toy: 1950s American Bricks, made of wood by Halsam in the US.

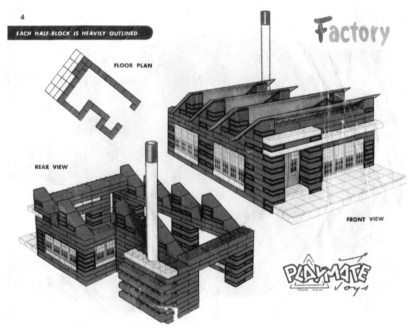

An Australian interlocking plastic brick toy of the 1960s: the Bilda-Brix Three-Storey House and the Factory from Set No. 2.

finished building to be picked up. Their designs, however, look much more 'architect designed' than the American ones.

The lack of lintels implies that the Elgo plastic bricks (like Lego, of which more later) interlocked sufficiently to hold together without lintels over the openings. Another interpretation is that you were not expected to build wide-span openings, thereby dismissing one of Le Corbusier's desired Five Points of Architecture, *la fenêtre en longueur* (the long horizontal window).[15]

Apart from the interlocking, another aspect of American Bricks is that they were designed for building cities. Indeed, Halsam and Elgo made all the components of a city and its hinterland. There were American Logs out in the sticks, American Bricks (either wooden or plastic) in the suburbs, and American Skyline, an Elgo set for making skyscrapers,[16] in the Central Business District. As Halsam's leaflet says, 'Many families buy set after set of…Bricks – permanent models are built at small expense – eventually complete…modern cities result.' The idea of building a city is of course a great way to sell more bricks, and thinking about sales success will bring us to Lego.

But before Lego there was Hilary Page, a British toy designer who founded a company called Kiddicraft in 1932, using his savings of £100.[17] He researched and wrote on child development, and was interested in using plastics to make toys because he was concerned about small children chewing the paint off wooden toys;[18] he introduced his 'Sensible Toys', made from plastics, in 1937.[19] Page marketed his new Kiddicraft Self-locking Building Bricks after the Second World War, when plastics became more widespread. He applied for a patent for these in 1944 and it was granted in 1947,[20] following an earlier patent for square bricks. The Self-locking Bricks were rectangular (brick shaped, in fact) with eight circular studs on the top, and look very like Lego. They were not a great success for Kiddicraft, or at least not a major part of their sales, and the company suffered further problems that may have been part of the reason for Page's suicide in 1957.[21]

In Billund, Denmark, in the 1930s the carpenter and joiner Ole Kirk Christiansen began making wooden toys, because the Depression had hit the building trade. Christiansen's quality toys were a success, and in 1934 he named his company Lego, a contraction of the Danish words *'Leg Godt'*, or 'play well', and, for Classical scholars, *to take out, pick out, extract, remove* (among other meanings) in Latin.[22] Certainly there is a lot of picking out and extracting involved in playing with Lego, accompanied by the distinctive sound of raking through the pieces like a cat in a litter tray. In 1947 Christiansen, who, like Page, saw that his future lay in plastics, bought an injection-moulding machine from a firm in London, and received with it, presumably to show what it could do, a sample of the Kiddicraft Self-locking bricks.[23] Lego soon made use of their new machine and came out with a copy of Page's bricks, called Automatic Binding Bricks,[24] but with some changes, as detailed in a court case that Lego later brought against a firm they accused of copying their design.[25]

Various firms subsequently made plastic bricks that were very like Lego, including Airfix, who are better known for their plastic model kits. The 1960s Airfix Betta Bilda[26] is definitely much harder to assemble than Lego[27] and it was initially designed only for making buildings, but it is one of the few building toys that makes a 'proper' roof, out of separate tiles. Like Wenebrik roofs, the Betta Bilda ones, which are green, are very hard to put together or to take apart.

Lego took the pirating of their bricks very seriously and back in 1987 were described as one of the most actively litigious companies in terms of intellectual property.[28] However, the result of their court case in 1988[29] has meant that copies of Lego bricks are no longer illegal, and there are now a number of versions that do the same sort of thing and that fit with genuine Lego, such as the Chinese 'Enlighten Brick'. However, Lego is still the authentic original product. The final part of Lego's current success was the 1958 redesign of the brick to incorporate tubes on the underside that improved its ability to stay connected (called 'clutch power' by Lego), with the result that all Lego bricks made since 1958 will still fit together with the company's most modern products. Over fifty years of production is an impressive record, rivalled only by Richter's Blocks and Meccano. The revised system for connecting Lego bricks also made it possible to manufacture sloping bricks,[30] which meant that one's toy houses were no longer obliged either to have flat roofs or look like ziggurats.

Even before the revised brick design, Lego were busy thinking about urban schemes, and in a key decision the bricks, which had become *Lego Mursten* (Lego Bricks) in 1953, became in 1955 the *Lego Mursten System i Leg* (Lego Bricks System of Play).[31] Here Lego did for toy bricks what Märklin had done in the nineteenth century for toy trains: they made a system. Halsam had suggested building a city by using lots of American Bricks, implying that a city is formed when two or three houses come together. Lego, on the other hand, applied the principles of municipal planning and made not just houses but a whole scheme capable of

An early version of classic Lego: 1950 Lego Automatic Binding Bricks, Denmark.

A 1960s British interlocking brick toy by Airfix called Betta Bilda, which had very fiddly interlocking roof tiles.

expansion, which included a vinyl play mat printed with a town plan and roads, a series of residential and commercial buildings to put on it, and a church, plus a range of plastic cars, lorries, trees, bushes and road signs.[32]

The advantage for Lego, as it had been for Märklin, was that a system offered continuing sales. A system also provided a selection of items at different prices: you could use your pocket money to add a single car to your city while waiting for a kindly relative to give you a big set of bricks for your birthday. In architectural terms, this Lego city of 1955 has a relatively modern appearance, which makes it look like the first of Britain's postwar New Towns, such as Stevenage with its pedestrianized city centre.[33] Scandinavian (and hence Danish) design is cited as one of the influences on the British New Towns: the reason why they looked different from what had gone before,[34] and presumably the reason why they look like Lego.

Moving to the twenty-first century, which has not turned out to be nearly as futuristic as we thought it would be in the 1950s, the call is now more for green cities than for New Towns. The *European Green City Index*, a recent study of thirty cities in Europe, found that while cities were striving to be green, they were still a long way from getting there, with only 7.3% of total energy from renewable sources, only 20% of waste recycled, and nearly 25% of water lost through leakage.[35] The 'greenest' city overall was deemed to be Copenhagen,[36] whose goals include becoming the first capital city in the world to be carbon neutral by 2025.[37] Lego is a proudly Danish company, so if Denmark's capital is Europe's greenest city, maybe Lego also follows this green trend.

Lego's *Progress Report 2011*, which deals with sustainability, tells how the company organized an event in Melbourne called 'Build the Change', in which 800 Australian schoolchildren built a green city out of Lego.[38] Without being entirely specific about it, because Lego has never marketed a 'Green City', Lego has over the years managed to provide some of its components. The *European Green City Index* measures cities' greenness in the fields of CO_2, Energy, Buildings, Transport, Water, Waste and land use, Air Quality and Environmental Governance.[39] If we assume that those little Lego people (officially called 'Minifigures') are not capable of much in the way of Environmental Governance, what does Lego offer in the other fields? How does it reproduce, on the carpet, the kinds of cities that would be desirably green in real life?

Between 2008 and 2011 Lego made five sets that seem to form essential components of the green city. The first is the 'Construction Site' (no. 7633), in which a large mobile crane is the centrepiece of a block of low-rise medium-density apartments with shops on the ground floor. The flats are prefabricated in room-sized modules and the crane boom is long enough for them to be stacked up to four storeys high, but not higher, so the Lego Minifigures can walk up and don't need a lift. This one is perhaps a bit hard to describe as particularly green, but medium-density housing often figures in proposals for greener development – for example, it forms part of the Green Party of New Zealand's housing policy in an attempt to improve public transport access and avoid urban sprawl.[40] The next, undeniably green, set, released in 2009, is called 'Wind Turbine Transport' (no. 7747). It makes a large-scale wind turbine to power the green city and a truck and trailer to transport it from the factory to the site where it is to be put up (perhaps with the aid of the previous year's crane?).

The year 2010 produced the apotheosis of urban sustainability, the 'Public Transport Station' (no. 8404), a set that includes not only a bus and a tram, but also a street-sweeping vehicle, a bus/tram interchange station, a bus or tram stop with cycle rack and bike, a kiosk for buying postcards, a couple of recycling bins and a sports car – this last is not very green but maybe it is a hybrid, and we have to hope that the bus is bio-diesel or battery-powered. Also in 2010, there was the 'City House', a three-storey residence using the same prefabricated elements as the original apartments, but designed as a town house, and with the inclusion of a small photovoltaic panel on the roof. There is another Lego set of a house with a solar panel on the roof, the 'Hillside House' (no. 5771), introduced in 2011, but it is not part of the City range. Lego, in these five sets, have covered CO_2 and Energy with the wind turbine set, Transport, Waste and maybe Air Quality with the public transport set, and Buildings with the Construction Site, City House and Hillside House.

In the real material world, Lego is made from acrylonitrile butadiene styrene plastic (ABS), which is made from oil and natural gas.[41] In 2011 Lego used 49,000 tonnes of plastic, which is actually relatively little material.[42] It takes the equivalent of 2 kilograms (4½ lbs) of oil to make 1 kilogram (2¼ lbs) of ABS,[43] so the manufacture of Lego currently uses roughly 100,000 tonnes of oil a year. A typical Lego set from the ones listed above to form the green city weighs less than 2 kilograms, so the whole green city in Lego would represent less than 20 kilograms (44 lbs) of oil equivalent. In measurements of energy consumption, a kilogram of oil equivalent represents roughly 42MJ.[44] An average car will use around 3MJ per kilometre (⅔ mile) over its lifetime[45] so the Lego green city

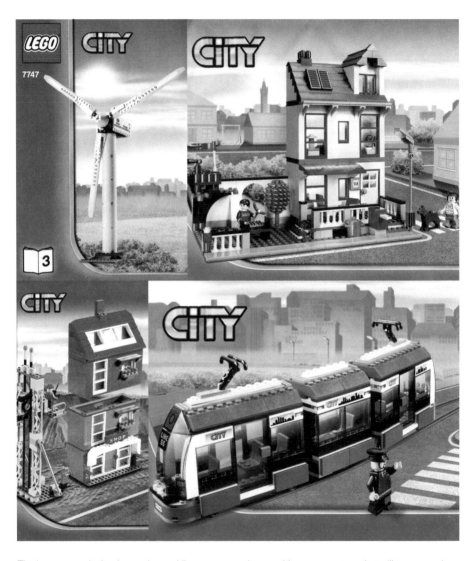

The Lego green city has low-carbon public transport and renewable-energy systems, but still too many dogs.

would represent 840MJ or 280 kilometres (174 miles) of driving. This is probably the same distance you might drive to go and buy the Lego sets one by one from an out-of-town retail centre. By comparison, a modern soldier uses 1,080MJ (25 kilograms/55lbs) of oil a day.[46] Among all the other things that are done with oil, making Lego out of it seems pretty blameless, not least because Lego bricks are so durable and emit no greenhouse gases during use.

The United Kingdom's first Autonomous House (1993), which was in the middle of a town but provided all its services from sun and rain, was made entirely from off-the-shelf materials and components.[47] Such houses could form one element of a green city. One of the nice points about the Lego version of the green city is that, like the Autonomous House, all the models are made out of standard pre-existing Lego parts. We do not need to invent anything new, either in Lego or in reality, to build the green city, we just need to choose to do it. A Lego green city can be created from available Lego sets, if you are prepared to search them out. The Lego version even has all the attributes of the *European Green City Index*, with its wind and solar energy systems, its public transport and waste recycling, its bicycles and medium-density housing.

However, the Lego version of the green city can be considered only as green as the real ones, which means not very green at all. Out of the thirty cities around Europe studied in the *European Green City Index*, the carbon dioxide emissions per head of the city population range from a relatively commendable 2.19 tonnes per year in Oslo to a slightly scary 9.72 tonnes per year in Dublin, but even Oslo can be described merely as 'greener' rather than green. After all, 2.19 tonnes is a lot for one person: it is 6 kilograms (13 lbs) a day, although nothing like as bad as the nearly 27 kilograms (60 lbs, or over 4 stone) of CO_2 a day thrown into the atmosphere by the average Dubliner. By comparison, Norway's more tangible municipal waste per capita is 800 kilograms (⅘ tonne) a year, or only about 2.2 kilograms (5 lbs) a day, and Norway, along with Ireland, is the worst producer of waste in the OECD (Organisation for Economic Co-operation and Development).[48] People tend to worry about municipal waste because you can see it, but carbon dioxide is invisible and so not considered an immediate problem, even though Europe's lowest-CO_2-emitting city produces three times as much of it by weight as it does solid garbage. The conclusion is that Oslo is indeed better than Dublin, but it has a very long way to go before it could be considered green.

The Lego green city reflects the token gestures of the real ones. Yes, the houses have solar panels, but houses with a solar panel or two on the roof do not have nearly enough solar input to make a useful contribution to the energy demand of the house. To stand a chance of producing enough electricity to run a typical modern household you need to cover the whole roof with solar panels. Perhaps an even bigger issue is that both the Lego houses that have solar panels on the roof come with a plastic dog. Research has shown that the environmental impact of even a medium-sized real dog rivals that of a big four-wheel drive SUV.[49] So it is no good putting a solar panel on the roof and then having a dog, even if you take the Lego tram to work. This shows that serious 'greening' of cities is going to demand some difficult decisions. Indeed, it looks as if cities in the future are in for some pretty hard times.[50]

CHAPTER FIFTEEN

Learning Architecture on the Carpet

OES ARCHITECTURE DRIVE THE TOY or does the toy reflect the architecture of the time? Or even – in Bilt-E-Z's emphatic slogan – does 'The Toy Build The Boy': that is, does the type of construction toy affect the inclinations and capabilities of the child who uses it? At the start of this journey we had thought the answers would be clear by its end, but now we are less sure. It does seem that modernism was pushed through in the marketing of railway accessories for those playing with Hornby and Trix railways. However, what of those playing with the cheaper Tri-ang sets, which stuck to the Victorian image of the railways until the 1960s? Was modernism only for the wealthy and middle classes? Perhaps it is architecture that is only for those who have money – they can choose their architecture, but those without must put up with what they are given. Certainly sets such as Arkitex, with their limited outcomes, are a true reflection of what happens when the modernist building is both prefabricated and cheap – the outcomes are repetitive. Lott's Bricks, however, with a reasonably limited palette do so much more simply because the module is so small, whereas the storey-height panel of Arkitex is much more restrictive. So maybe construction toys have much to teach about the nature of prefabrication.

As to building the boy (and as we've seen, it was usually a boy), something about the aesthetic appeal and clarity of function of Meccano does seem to have influenced notable architects including Norman Foster and Richard Rogers (see

Chapter 3), though playing with Arkitex does not seem to have given such critics as Jonathan Glancey an enduring love for the modern office block. Something about the abilities encouraged by building on the carpet can also be learned from the instruction books. There does seem to be a 'dumbing down' when it comes to modern toys. Lego is meticulous in giving brick-by-brick instructions, usually in a three-dimensional projection, coloured, of each finished building stage. Earlier toys like Richter's Blocks and Minibrix would give a list of all bricks required and a view of the finished building, though in some cases key stages or plan layouts were given as well. Meccano, although they list the parts required for each model, are perhaps most notorious for their lack of instructions, with the classic injunction 'The construction of the lifeboat itself is clear from the various illustrations'.[1] Since the sequence of putting the strips, nuts and bolts together is often vital, there is a degree of trial and error involved in most Meccano models, thus mirroring the basic engineering approach of 'have a go and if it doesn't work try something different'. Since much modern building is to do with assembly of factory-made parts rather than craftsmanship on site, maybe Lego does no more than reflect the general level of ability required in the building industry. Perhaps engineers really are made in the nursery, which is why people bemoan, for example, the decline in British engineering.

In a consumer society, producing the new is the way to keep us buying; the change in toys after the Second World War, and the fact they moved from generic systems to sets that would build particular models, is a reflection of this. Indeed, this trend appeared to start with Juneero during the war. However, the generic box of bricks can still bring out the best in most of us. Because we were writing this book, a friend sent us an old set of French wooden bricks for Christmas. Immediately our five-year-old grand-daughter and her PhD mathematician uncle sat down on the carpet and started trying to build the highest and most beautiful tower possible. It kept them occupied for a long time. As long as we can stack we can build, and as long as we can build there will be architecture. Building toys are just one step along that path.

Notes

INTRODUCTION: TOYS ARE US

1 W. Wordsworth, 'My Heart Leaps Up When I Behold' (1802)

2 M. Seaborne and R. Lowe, *The English School* (London: Routledge and Kegan Paul, 1977), p. 4.

3 F. Froebel and W. N. Hailmann (transl.), *The Education of Man* (New York: D. Appleton-Century, 1887), p. 285.

4 H. Page, *Playtime in the First Five Years* (Croydon: Watson and Crossland Ltd, 1938).

5 In 1916 a zoning ordinance required step backs to ensure there was sufficient daylight at street level.

CHAPTER ONE: MODERNISM ON THE LINE

1 http://www.marklin.com/about/about2.html (viewed 10 May 2012).

2 http://www.lionel.com/CentralStation/LionelPastAndPresent/ (viewed 10 May 2012).

3 http://www.historyhome.co.uk/peel/railways/expans.htm (viewed 5 May 2011).

4 P. Carlson, *Toy Trains: A history* (London: Victor Gollancz Ltd, 1986).

5 http://www.marklin.com/about/about2.html (viewed 5 May 2011).

6 http://www.tcawestern.org/marklin.htm

7 Celebrated, for example, in the 300 km long 'German toy road' tourist route in http://www.guide-to-bavaria.com/en/German-Toy-Road.html (viewed 5 May 2011).

8 Carlson, *Toy Trains: A History*, pp. 75–79.

9 Ibid., pp. 92–101.

10 K. D. Brown, *Factory of Dreams: A history of Meccano Ltd* (Lancaster: Crucible Books, 2007).

11 J. R. Hastings, 'Famous English Railway Stations', *The New Zealand Railways Magazine,* 10(1), April 1935, p. 49.

12 R. Thorne, *Liverpool Street Station* (London: Academy Editions, 1978), p. 44.

13 Total miles of track open in 1865 were around 11,000 and the system had expanded to around 18,000 miles by 1900. Maximum size was just over 20,000 miles, reached in 1925. Data from the Science Museum, London at http://www.makingthemodernworld.org.uk/learning modules/history/04.TU.03/?style=expander_popup&filename=expandables/04.EX.09.xml

14 See, for example, the 1931 Lionel and American Flyer ranges in Supplee-Biddle's *1931 Toy Catalog from Philadelphia's Wholesale Toy Headquarters* (Philadelphia, Pa.: Supplee-Biddle Hardware Co., 1931), pp. IC 1–6.

15 R. Fuller (ed.), *The Bassett-Lowke Story* (London: New Cavendish Books, 1984).

16 *78 Derngate – A History – Part 6: The 1916/17 transformation* available at http://www.78derngate.org.uk/content/78-derngate-history-part-6 (viewed 20 May 2011).

17 Howarth quoted in R. Billcliffe, *Charles Rennie Mackintosh: The complete furniture, furniture drawings and interior designs* (Guildford: Lutterworth Press, 1979), p. 218.

18 Ibid., p. 222.

19 G. Stamp, 'He wasn't seduced', *The Spectator,* 1 February 1997.

20 A. Windsor, *Peter Behrens Architect and Designer* (London: The Architectural Press, 1981), pp. 162–63.

21 Ibid., pp. 77–82.

22 Ibid., p. 102.

23 S. Giedion, *Mechanisation Takes Command* (New York: Oxford University Press, 1948), p. 484.

24 N. Levy, 'W. J. Bassett-Lowke as Architectural Patron' in Fuller, *The Bassett-Lowke Story,* pp. 67–74.

25 Windsor, *Peter Behrens Architect and Designer,* p. 162.

26 http://www.britishlistedbuildings.co.uk/en-232253-new-ways-508-northampton/bingmap (viewed 20 May 2011).

27 Fuller, *The Bassett-Lowke Story,* p. 37.

28 Anon, 'Names of the four grouped companies', *The Railway Gazette,* 24 November 1922, p. 641.

29 'At the British Industries Fair, Messrs Trix were showing…a full range of samples of the new "Many-Ways" Station Buildings…They have been designed by Mr. E. W. Twining on the lines of the modern Southern Railway Stations now being built.' Anon, 'Latest Developments in Model Railways' *Newnes Popular Mechanics,* April 1937, p. 394.

30 http://glostransporthistory.visit-gloucestershire.co.uk/rail.htm (viewed 22 May 2011).

31 http://www.hoteldesigns.co.uk/review/review_359_1.html (viewed 22 May 2011).

32 http://www.bbc.co.uk/lancashire/content/articles/2008/06/11/places_midland_hotel_history_feature.shtml (viewed 20 May 2011).

33 http://en.wikipedia.org/wiki/Chessington_Branch_Line (viewed 21 May 2011).

34 Surbiton Station is on the National Monuments Record of English Heritage http://www.imagesofengland.org.uk/details/default.aspx?id=203194 (viewed 21 May 2011).

35 http://www.michaeltaylor.ca/old/sr-infra.htm (viewed 21 May 2011).

36 C. Barman, *The Man Who Built London Transport: A biography of Frank Pick* (Newton Abbott: David and Charles, 1979), p. 118.

37 E. Karol and F. Allibone, *Charles Holden: Architect 1875–1960* (Westerham, Kent: Westerham Press, 1988), p. 25.

CHAPTER TWO: RICHTER'S BLOCKS AND THE CASTLES ON THE RHINE

1 Production ran from 1880 to 1963, when the East German government closed the factory, but was revived in 1995: http://www.ankerstein.de/ (viewed 10 May 2011).

2 G. Hardy, *Richter's Anchor Stone Building Sets* (Charlottesville, Va.: George Hardy, 2007).

3 http://www.anchorblocks.co.uk/history.html (12 March 2009).

4 *Richter Villa and Factory*, at http://www.ankerstein. ch/org/2001/06/bldr.htm (viewed 14 June 2011).

5 Club Van Ankervrienden, *Anker-Bausteine*, (Den Haag: CVA, 1999), pp. 1-101-1-122.

6 Einpackvorlagen GK-NF, http://cva.flying-cat.de (viewed 14 June 2011).

7 VEB Gernegross Set, http://cva.flying-cat.de/ Vorlagen/VEB/GERNEGRO/1.JPG (viewed 14 June 2011).

8 A. Kopisch, *Geditchte* (Berlin: Verlag von Dunder und Humblot, 1836), poem 195.

9 R. Southey, *The Poetical Works of Robert Southey* (London: Longman, Orme, Brown, Green, and Longmans, 1838), vol. 6, pp. 57–60.

10 G. Rees, *The Rhine* (London: Weidenfeld and Nicolson, 1967), pp. 113–14.

11 Plans to build the Mouse Tower in Richter Blocks can be found at http://www.ankerstein.ch/ downloads/CVA/12.pdf (viewed 14 June 2011).

12 UNESCO, Upper Middle Rhine valley, *World Heritage Convention*, http://whc.unesco.org/en/ list/1066 (viewed 14 June 2011).

13 P. Blickle, *Heimat: A critical theory of the German idea of homeland* (Rochester, NY: Camden House, 2002), p. 48.

14 Ibid., p. 51.

15 D. Blackbourn and G. Eley, *The Peculiarities of German History: Bourgeois society and politics in nineteenth-century Germany* (Oxford: Oxford University Press, 1984), p. 214.

16 Charles Dickens, *The Pickwick Papers* (Oxford: Clarendon Press, 1986; first published 1836), p. 6.

17 P. S. Bagwell, *The Transport Revolution from 1770* (London: Batsford, 1974), p. 125.

18 P. A. Yougman, *Black Devil and Iron Angel: The railway in nineteenth-century German realism* (Washington DC: Catholic University of America Press, 2005), p. 42.

19 Hardy, *Richter's Anchor Stone Building Sets*, p. 117.

20 J. Ruskin, *The Seven Lamps of Architecture* (London: J. M. Dent, 1907; first published 1849), pp. 199–201.

21 http://en.wikipedia.org/wiki/File:Schloss_ Stolzenfels_Sammlung_Duncker.jpg (viewed 16 June 2011).

22 R. R. Taylor, *The Castles of the Rhine: Recreating the Middle Ages in modern Germany* (Waterloo, Ontario: Wilfrid Laurier University Press, 1998), p. 134.

23 Ibid., p. 129.

24 A. Bernhard et al., *Karl Frederick Schinkel: Guide to his buildings* (Munich and Berlin: Deutscher Kunstverlag, 2007), pp. 9–11.

25 Ibid., p. 348.

26 http://en.wikipedia.org/wiki/File:Burg_ Lahneck_2010.jpg (viewed 14 June 2011).

27 Taylor, *The Castles of the Rhine: Recreating the middle ages in modern Germany*, p.173.

28 http://www.feiertagsgedichte.de/autoren/g/ goethe/erstes-buch/geistes-gruss/geistes-gruss. html (viewed 14 June 2011).

29 UNESCO, *World Heritage Convention*: http:// www.welterbe-oberes-mittelrheintal.info/index. php?id=41&L=3 (viewed 15 June 2011).

30 I. Feuerlicht, 'Heine's Lorelei: Legend, literature, life', *The German Quarterly* 53(1), 1980, pp. 84–86.

31 V. Hugo, *The Rhine* (London: Colburn, 1843), Ch. XVII.

32 J. Hermand, R. C. Holub (eds), *Poetry and Prose: Heinrich Heine* (New York: The Continuum Publishing Company, 1982), p. viii.

33 S. R. Hauer, Wagner and the 'Völospá', *19th-Century Music* 15(1), 1991, pp. 52–63.

34 R. Sternberg, 'Fantasy, Geography, Wagner, and Opera', *Geographical Review* 88(3), 1998, pp. 327–30.

35 P. Carnegy, *Wagner and the Art of the Theatre* (New Haven: Yale University Press, 2006), p. 43.

36 Debrett, Cooper-Hewitt, V&A Museum, *Designs for the Dream King* (London: Debrett's Peerage Ltd, 1978), plates 6, 7 and 22.

37 Ibid., p. 66.

38 P. Warde, 'Fear of Wood Shortage and the Reality of the Woodland in Europe', *c.*1450–1850, *History Workshop Journal* 62(1), 2006, pp. 28–57.

39 Blickle, *Heimat: A critical theory of the German idea of homeland*, p. 115.

CHAPTER THREE: MECCANO AND MAKING VISIBLE HOW THINGS WORK

1 K. Brown, *Factory of Dreams: A history of Meccano Ltd, 1901–1979* (Lancaster: Crucible Books, 2007), pp. 27–34.

2 W. Irwin, 'Meccano Geared Roller Bearing *c.*1937', International Society of Meccanomen (June 2001), available at http:// www.internationalmeccanomen.org.uk/ REFERENCES/CollandHistseries/GRB/grb. htm (viewed 6 September 2011)

3 E. H. Phelps Brown and S. Hopkins, 'Seven Centuries of Building Wages', *Economica*, New Series 22(87), August 1955, pp. 195–206.

4 Irwin, *Meccano Geared Roller Bearing c 1937*.

5 B. Love and J. Gamble, *The Meccano System and the Special Purpose Meccano Sets* (London: New Cavendish Books, 1986), p. 195.

6 B. Vale, *Prefabs* (London: E. and F. N. Spon, 1995).

7 Meccano Manuals to download, and much else

besides, are available from the 'Gallery' section of the New Zealand Meccano website www.nzmeccano.com (viewed 14 April 2012).

8 Anon., 'Off the Beaten Track', *Meccano Magazine*, September 1931), pp. 736–37.

9 R. S. Draper, 'Among the Model Buildings', *Meccano Magazine* October 1975, pp. 98–99.

10 J. Lichfield, 'Deconstructing Meccano: The story of a British icon', *The Independent*, Saturday 10 April (2010) at http://www.independent.co.uk/news/world/europe/deconstructing-meccano-the-story-of-a-british-icon-1940749.html (viewed 6 September 2011)

11 http://designmuseum.org/design/richard-rogers (viewed 6 September 2011).

12 D. Sudjic, *Norman Foster: A life in architecture* (London: Weidenfeld and Nicholson, 2010), pp. 25–26.

13 J. Kron and S. Slesin, *High Tech: The industrial style and source book for the home*, (New York: Clarkson N. Potter, 1978).

14 C. Davies, *High Tech Architecture* (New York: Rizzoli, 1988), p. 6.

15 Love and Gamble, *The Meccano System and the Special Purpose Meccano Sets*, p. 98.

16 Ibid., p. 51.

17 B. Huber and J-C. Steinegger, *Jean Prouvé: Prefabrication: Structures and Elements* (London: Pall Mall Press, 1971), pp. 76–77 (translation by R. Vale).

18 Ibid., pp. 98–101.

19 Ibid., p. 180.

20 Ibid., p. 88.

21 'Look Boys! You can build this TANK with Meccano' advertisement in *Boys' Life: The Boy Scouts' Magazine* 7(9), November 1917, p. 66.

22 J. Coogan, 'I have been a Meccano fan since I got my first set', *Popular Mechanics* Chicago, January 1926, p. 165.

23 R. Rogers and R. Piano, 'A Statement', *Architectural Design*, February 1977, p. 87.

24 Kron and Slesin, *High-Tech: the Industrial Style and Source Book for the Home*, p. 33.

25 Huber and Steinegger, *Jean Prouvé: Prefabrication: Structures and Elements*, p. 189.

26 D. Sudjic, *Norman Foster, Richard Rogers, James Stirling: New Directions in British Architecture* (London: Thames and Hudson, 1986), p. 180.

27 http://www.bbc.co.uk/history/british/victorians/iron_bridge_01.shtml (viewed 10 September 2011).

28 S. Fox, *The Ocean Railway* (London: Harper Perennial, 2003), p. 70.

29 Ibid., pp. 70–83.

30 Ibid., p. 62.

31 C. H. Gibbs-Smith, *The Great Exhibition of 1851: A commemorative album* (London: Victoria & Albert Museum and HMSO, 1950).

32 All information about the Crystal Palace from Ibid.

33 Love and Gamble, *The Meccano System and the Special Purpose Meccano Sets*, pp. 116–19.

34 Sudjic, *Norman Foster, Richard Rogers, James Stirling: New Directions in British Architecture*.

35 R. O'Neill, 'Meccano "Dam Busters" Computer stars at MOTAT', *Computerworld*, 16 July 2007, at http://computerworld.co.nz/news.nsf/tech/7627 BB58BAFE998DCC257317001AA6D1 (viewed 9 June 2011).

36 Gibbs-Smith, *The Great Exhibition of 1851: A commemorative album*, p. 26.

37 I. Nicholls, 'The Issigonis Gallery', 16 May 2011 at *Austin Rover On-line* at http://www.aronline.co.uk/index.htm?issiinterf.htm (viewed 9 June 2011).

38 BBC Shropshire, 'Shropshire Meccano modeller wins top prize', 8 July 2010 at http://news.bbc.co.uk/local/shropshire/hi/people_and_places/nature/newsid_8798000/8798799.stm (viewed 9 June 2011).

39 'Harold Kroto – Autobiography'. Nobelprize.org. at http://nobelprize.org/nobel_prizes/chemistry/laureates/1996/kroto-autobio.html (viewed 9 June 2011).

CHAPTER FOUR: LOTT'S BRICKS AND THE ARTS AND CRAFTS MOVEMENT

1 G. Brich, *Lott's Bricks* (Bushey: Bushey Museum Trust, 2008), pp. 5–6.

2 T. Schiemann, 'The United States and the War Cloud in Europe', *The American Review of Reviews*, 42(1), July 1910, http://www.oldmagazinearticles.com/pdf/Pre-War,-R.-of-Rs,2-pages.pdf (viewed 10 June 2011).

3 K. D. Brown, *Factory of Dreams* (Lancaster: Crucible Books, 2007), pp. 40–41.

4 B. Salter, *Building Toys* (Oxford: Shire Publications, 2011), p. 13.

5 G. White, *Antique Toys*, (London: Chancellor Press, 1971), p. 142.

6 Anon, 'Concrete Building on the Unit Principle', *Architectural Review* 45, January 1919, p. 66.

7 W. Morris, *News from Nowhere* (London: Routledge and Kegan Paul, 1970 ed., first pub. 1891), p. 137.

8 Ibid., p. 180.

9 Ibid., p. 19.

10 Ibid., p. 62.

11 Ibid., p. 123.

12 Ibid., p. 6, p. 179.

13 Ibid., pp. 34–35.

14 Ibid., p. 59.

15 C. Williams-Ellis, *Portmeirion: The place and its meaning*, (Penrhyndeudraeth: Portmeirion Ltd, 1973), p. 22.

16 M. Richardson, *Architects of the Arts and Crafts Movement*, (London: Trefoil Books, 1983), p. 59.

17 H. P. G. Maule, 'Some Recent Architectural Designs by Arnold Mitchell', *International Studio*, 18 January 1903 p. 179.

18 Ibid. which shows designs for houses in Northolt, Northwood, Great Stanmore, Rickmansworth and Harrow.

19 Anon., 'Architecture and Applied Art at the 'Ideal Home' Exhibition', *The Builder*, 31 October 1908, p. 454.

20 H. Muthesius, *Das Englische Haus* translated as *The English House*, (London: Frances Lincoln Ltd, 2007; first published 1904) vol. 1 of 3, pp. 162–63.

21 G. A. T. Middleton, *Modern buildings: their planning, construction and equipment*, (London: The Caxton Publishing Company, 1906), vol. 1, part 2, p. 38.

22 J. St. L. Strachey, *The Adventure of Living: A subjective autobiography*, (London: Hodder and Stoughton, 1922), at http://www.knowledgerush.com/paginated_txt/etext04/dvnlv10/dvnlv10_s1_p486_pages.html (viewed 20 June 2011).

23 L. Weaver, *The 'Country Life' Book of Cottages costing from £150 to £600*, (London: Country Life Ltd, 1913), p. 21.

24 http://www.gardencitymuseum.org/sites/default/files/Prizewinners.pdf (viewed 10 May 2012).

25 L. Weaver, *The 'Country Life' Book of Cottages*, (London: Country Life Ltd, 1919, 2nd edn), pp. 12–15.

26 Anon, 1913, 'Rural Housing' and 'A Cottage for £110', *The Times*, 18 Oct 1913, p. 12colA

27 Cottages were built in 1915 at Well Hall Estate, Woolwich by the Office of Works for munition workers and The London County Council built cottages estates such as those of Tooting and Tottenham; see G. Allen, *The Cheap Cottage and Small House*, (London: Batsford, 1919), pp. 38–41 and pp. 124–25.

28 L. Lambourne, *Utopian Craftsmen* (London: Astragal Books, 1980), pp. 124–36.

29 E. R. Robson, *School Architecture* (New York: Leicester University press, 1972; first published 1874), p. 301.

30 Slater, *Building Toys*, p. 17.

31 Lott's also made puzzle sets and games using pieces made of the same material as the bricks.

32 F. Jackson, *Sir Raymond Unwin: Architect, Planner and Visionary*, (London: A. Zwemmer Ltd, 1985), p. 95.

33 L. D. Abbot, 'William Morris's Commonweal', *The New England Magazine* 20(4), June 1899, pp. 428–33.

34 N. Pevsner, *Pioneers of Modern Design* (Harmondsworth: Penguin Books Ltd, 1960), p. 32.

35 Ibid., p. 217.

36 Morris, *News from Nowhere*, pp. 169–171.

CHAPTER FIVE: WENEBRIK AND THE (UN-MODERN) STEEL HOUSE

1 N. Jackson, *The Modern Steel House* (London: E. and F. N. Spon, 2000), pp. 3–5.

2 R. Sheppard, *Prefabrication in Building* (London: The Architectural Press, 1946), p. 39.

3 Vintage Bargains, *TinToy History* 2010 at http://www.virtualbargains.com/tintoyhistory/ (viewed 3 August 2011).

4 Bilt E-Z is a later American all-metal construction set that made buildings based on assembling the wall, roof and floor sections into cubes, hence providing a more modern aesthetic; see Ch. 12. http://www.architoys.net/toys/toypages/biltez.html (viewed 3 August 2011). Other sets of metal panels had tabs along the edges which could be joined as a hinge by threading through rods, for example the Meccano-made Dinky Builder, see http://www.architoys.net/toys/toylist1.html (viewed 3 August 2011).

5 'William Bailey (Birmingham)', Grace's Guide: http://www.gracesguide.co.uk/William_Bailey_(Birmingham) (viewed 3 August 2011).

6 Advertisement in *The Children's Newspaper* 611, 6 December 1930, p. 15. This same edition of the paper carries advertisements for Hornby Trains and Meccano and was for the relatively well-off child. There are many articles and advertisements encouraging the child towards philanthropic giving for the Christmas season.

7 Anon., *A Short History of Metal Constructional Systems 1888–1918* at http://www.osnl.co.uk/history%20web%20to%201918.htm (viewed 4 August 2011.)

8 M. Caird, *Mollie Caird's reminiscences of her childhood* n.d. at http://www.molliecaird.com/Mollie's%20reminiscences.html (viewed 4 August 2011).

9 Anon., Advertising leaflet: 'The New Meccano: Beautifully enamelled in colours – bigger outfits, new parts, more models' (Liverpool: Meccano Ltd, 1926).

10 N. Pevsner, *A History of Building Types* (London: Thames and Hudson, 1976), p. 276.

11 G. Herbert, *Pioneers of Prefabrication* (Baltimore: The John Hopkins University Press, 1978), pp. 97–109.

12 I. Smith, *Tin Tabernacles: Corrugated iron mission halls, churches and chapels of Britain* (Pembroke: Camrose, 2004).

13 Le Corbusier, Trans Etchells. *Towards a New Architecture* (London: Architectural Press, 1927), p. 123.

14 R. Sheppard, *Cast Iron in Building* (London: George Allen and Unwin, 1945), p. 71; R. Sheppard, *Prefabrication in Building*, J. Madge, *Tomorrow's Houses* (London: Pilot Press, 1945), pp. 114–15.

15 B. Kelly, *The Prefabrication of Houses* (New York: The Technology Press of MIT and John Wiley and Sons, Inc., 1951), p. 8.

16 Black Country History, *'Toll End bridge', Dudley No. 2 Canal, Windmill End Junction, Netherton*, n.d. at http://blackcountryhistory.org/collections/getrecord/GB145_p_2206/ (viewed 4 August 2011).

17 Anon, *Tintern: Heritage listed location*, n.d. at http://www.onmydoorstep.com.au/heritage-listing/1079/tintern (viewed 10 September 2011).

18 National Trust of Australia, *Corio Villa – Geelong*, n.d. at http://www.nattrust.com.au/heritage_accommodation/bay_beach_and_surf/corio_villa_geelong (viewed 4 August 2011).

19 W. R. Brownhill, *The History of Geelong and Corio Bay* (Melbourne: Wilke and Co., 1955), p. 118.

20 Ibid., p. 215.

21 Ibid., p. 618.

22 N. Thompson, *Corrugated Iron Buildings* (Oxford: Shire Publications, 2011), pp. 7–8.

23 M. Higgs, 'The Exported Iron Buildings of Andrew Handyside and Co. of Derby', *Journal of the Society of Architectural Historians* 29(2), May 1970, pp. 175–80.

24 A. Mornement and S. Holloway, *Corrugated Iron: Building on the frontier* (London: Frances Lincoln Ltd, 2007), p. 109.

25 An example is Tahurangi House, NZ. This prefabricated barracks was made in Melbourne *c.*1855 and imported to NZ to house soldiers at New Plymouth during the unrest between Maori and Pakeha over land sales 1854–55, see http://www.doc.govt.nz/conservation/historic/by-region/taranaki/north-egmont-camphouse/ (viewed 4 August 2011).

26 G. Herbert, *The Dream of the Factory Made House* (Cambridge: The MIT Press, 1984), p. 1.

27 A. Hassam, *Through Australian Eyes: Colonial perceptions of imperial Britain,* (Melbourne: Melbourne University Press, 2000), p. 54.

28 Ibid., p. 57.

29 Ibid., pp. 52–53, 193.

30 Le Corbusier, *Towards a New Architecture* (London: The Architectural Press, 1946; first published 1927), pp. 210, 250; J. Gloag and G. Wornum, *House out of Factory* (London: George Allen and Unwin, 1946), p. 5; J. and M. Fry, *Architecture for Children* (London: George Allen and Unwin, 1944), pp. 70–72.

31 Ministry of Works, *Post-war Building Studies No. 1: House Construction* (London: HMSO, 1944), p. 7; M. Bowley, *The British Building Industry* (Cambridge: Cambridge University Press, 1966), pp. 199–207.

32 M. Pawley, *Design Heroes: Buckminster Fuller* (London: Grafton, 1992), pp. 44–52.

33 J. Meller (ed.), *The Buckminster Fuller Reader* (London: Jonathon Cape, 1970), pp. 29–30.

34 Isaiah 2:4.

35 Kelly, *The Prefabrication of Houses*, p. 26.

36 http://designmuseum.org/design/r-buckminster-fuller (viewed 11 August 2011).

37 H. W. Jandi, *Yesterday's Houses of Tomorrow* (Washington DC: The Preservation Press, 1991), pp. 40–53.

38 R. Buckminster Fuller 'Dymaxion House' *The Architectural Forum* 56, March 1932, pp. 285–88

39 Jandi, *Yesterday's Houses of Tomorrow*, p. 90.

40 J. Baldwin, *BuckyWorks,* (New York: John Wiley and Sons, 1996), p. 56.

41 Lustron Initiative, 'Welcome to Lustron Preservation!' at http://www.lustronpreservation.org/ (viewed 11 August 2011).

42 Adshead was the first Professor of Town Planning at Liverpool University (1909) and Abercrombie, who was later to succeed him, started as his assistant. Adshead later formed an architectural partnership with Stanley Ramsey working in Liverpool and London. See C. Reilly, *Representative British Architects of the Present Day* (London: Batsford, 1931), pp. 15-27.

43 C. Buckley, 'Modernity, Tradition and the Design of the "Industrial Village" of Dormanstown 1917–1923', *Journal of Design History* 23(1), 2010, pp. 21–41.

44 J. Nicholson, *Building the Sydney Harbour Bridge* (St Leonards, NSW: Allen and Unwin, 2000), p. 7.

45 Based on 1.5kg/m² steel framing and a 100m² house; see http://www.hi-tech.net.nz/faq.html (viewed 2 September 2011.)

46 R. B. White, *Prefabrication: A history of its development in Great Britain* (London: HMSO, 1965), pp. 74–76.

47 Ibid., p. 79.

48 Scottish Office Building Directorate, *A Guide to Non-traditional and Temporary Housing in Scotland 1923–1955* (Edinburgh: HMSO, 1987), pp. 239–42.

49 Ibid., pp. 53–54.

50 Ministry of Works, *Post-war Building Studies No. 1: House Construction* (London: HMSO, 1944), p. 89.

51 Official Report House of Lords 1943–44, vol. 130 col. 700.

52 Ministry of Works architect, C. J. Mole and consultant architect A. W. Kenyon.

53 B. Vale, *Prefabs: A history of the UK Temporary Housing Programme,* (London: E. and F. N. Spon, 1995), pp. 5–19 and 28.

54 National Association of Steel-framed Housing, *Nash Milestones*, 2009 at http://www.nash.asn.au/nash/nash-and-steel-framing/nash-milestones.html (viewed 10 September 2011).

55 R. J. Unstead and W. F. Henderson, *Pioneer Home Life in Australia,* (London: A&C Black Ltd, 1971), p. 43.

CHAPTER SIX: LINCOLN LOGS AND THE LOG CABIN

1 Cited by the cook in the Disney animated film *Atlantis: The lost empire* (2001).

2 http://www.knex.com/building_toys/commemorative_edition.php (viewed 12 May 2011).

3 P. Armstrong and D. Jackson, *Toys of Early New Zealand,* (Wellington: Grantham House, 1990), p. 62.

4 E. Cho, 'Lincoln Logs: Toying with the frontier myth', *History Today* 43, April 1993, p. 33.

5 F. L. Wright, *An Autobiography,* (London: Faber and Faber, 1945), p. 192.

6 J. L. Wright, *My Father, Frank Lloyd Wright,* (New York: Dover, 1992; first published 1946), p. 96.

7 Ibid., p. 102.

8 W. M. Thayer, *Abraham Lincoln: The pioneer boy and how he became president,* (London: Hodder and Stoughton, 1896), ch. 1.

9 W. M. Thayer, *From Log-cabin to White House,* (London: Ward, Lock and Co., 1920).

10 H. Beecher Stowe, *Uncle Tom's Cabin,* (Boston: John P. Jewett and Co., 1852), ch. 4 at http://etext.lib.virginia.edu/toc/modeng/public/StoCabi.html (viewed 12 May 2011).

11 http://cgi.ebay.com/1920-WRIGHT-First-Lincoln-Logs-Patent45968 (viewed 12 May 2011).

12 http://www.fundinguniverse.com/company-histories/Greyhound-Lines-Inc-Company-History.html (viewed 18 September 2011).

13 L. Plachno, 'Greyhound Buses through the Years: Part 1', *National Bus Trader,* September 2002, p. 20.

14 W. J. Macintire, *The Pioneer Log House in Kentucky* (Frankfort: Kentucky Heritage Council, 1998), p. 2; P. Cox and J. Freeland, *Rude Timber Buildings of Australia* (London: Thames and Hudson, 1969), p. 11.

15 H. Phelps and R. MacGregor (transl.), *The Craft of Log Building* (Ottawa: Lee Valley Tools Ltd, 1982), p. 3.

16 Ibid., pp. 135, 138.

17 R. G. Knapp, *China's Traditional Rural Architecture* (Honolulu: University of Hawaii Press, 1986), p. 64.

18 R. G. Knapp, *Chinese Houses: The architectural heritage of a nation* (North Clarendon, Vermont: Tuttle Publishing, 2005), p. 44.

19 D. and M. Young, *The Art of Japanese Architecture* (Tokyo: Tuttle Publishing, 2007), p. 134.

20 http://nla.gov.au/nla.pic-vn5149801 (viewed 18 September 2011).

21 Cox and Freeland, *Rude Timber Buildings of Australia,* p. 44.

22 Ibid., plates 5, 6 and 7 and p. 194.

23 R. Mayne, *Four Years in British Columbia and Vancouver Island: An account of their forests, rivers, coasts, gold fields, and resources for colonisation* (London: John Murray, 1862).

24 Ibid., p. 88.

25 A. W. Bealer and J. O. Ellis, *The Log Cabin* (Barre, Massachusetts: Barre Publishing, 1978), p. 10

26 Ibid., p. 11.

27 http://lincolnlogs.knex.com/customer/products.php?cat=355 (viewed 18 September 2011).

28 W. Wright, *Sixguns and Society* (Los Angeles: University of California Press, 1975), p. 15.

29 J. G. Cawelti, *The Six-gun* Mystique (Bowling Green Ohio: Bowling Green Popular Press, 1971), p. 82.

30 B. R. Burke in P. Varner (ed.), *Westerns: Paperback novels and movies from Hollywood* (Newcastle: Cambridge Scholars Publishing, 2007), p. 84–102.

31 R. Merlock in K. M. Jackson (ed.), *Rituals and Patterns in Children's Lives* (Wisconsin: University of Wisconsin Press, 2005), pp. 235–51.

32 J. Tuska, *The American West in Film,* (Lincoln: University of Nebraska Press, 1985), p. 18 and Plate 3.

33 http://www.lockwood.co.nz/Default.aspx?pageID=2145885538 (viewed 2 October 2011).

34 http://www.beehive.govt.nz/node/25440 (viewed 2 October 2011).

35 http://www.auboisjoli.com/au-bois-joli/b-construction-sets-jeujura-b-1745/maison-en-rondins.html (viewed 18 September 2011).

36 Anon, 'Les Jeux de Construction', *Jouet Mag!,* No. 6, September 2002, at http://www.musee-du-jouet.com/jouetmag/construction.pdf (viewed 18 September 2011).

37 http://www.oldhouseweb.com/how-to-advice/the-preservation-and-repair-of-historic-log-buildings.shtml (viewed 29 August 2011).

38 http://www.rurala.co.uk/02/ (viewed 3 October 2011).

39 W. A. Bruette, *Log Camps and Cabins* (New York: The Nessmuk Library, 1934), p. 6.

40 H. Thoreau, *Walden* (1854) in C. Bode (ed.), *The Portable Thoreau* (Harmondsworth: Penguin, 1982) pp. 296, 299.

CHAPTER SEVEN: MOBACO AND DE STIJL

1 J. J. Vriend, *The Amsterdam School* (Amsterdam: Meulenhoff, 1970).

2 http://www.panoramio.com/photo/47752372 (viewed 20 April 2012).

3 See http://mobaco.50webs.com/PartsLists/All.htm (viewed 2 November 2011).

4 http://www.miniplex.nl/default.htm (Viewed 2 November 2011).

5 http://www.collectobil.com/guide/1974.html (viewed 30 October 2011).

6 http://mobaco.50webs.com/Sets/Sets.htm (viewed 30 October 2011).

7 H. J. Louw, 'Anglo-Netherlandish architectural

interchange *c.*1600–*c.*1660', *Architectural History* 24, 1981, pp. 1–23 and 125–44.

8   K. Bayes, *Living Architecture,* (Hudson, NY: Anthroposophic Press and Floris Books, 1994), p. 11.

9   http://www.photographersdirect.com/buyers/ stockphoto.asp?imageid=3312636 (viewed 5 April 2012.)

10 F. R. Yerbury (ed.), *Old Domestic Architecture of Holland* (London: The Architectural Press, 1924), p. xii.

11 H. J. Louw, 'The origin of the sash-window', *Architectural History* 26, 1983, p. 49.

12 H. J. Louw and R. Crayford, 'A constructional history of the sash-window *c.*1670–*c.*1725', *Architectural History* 41, 1998, p. 83.

13 There exist a few other construction toys based on grooved uprights, often using thin wood panels, such as the American 'Bungalow Building Blocks', 'Little House Builder', and 'Fox Blox' see http://www.architoys.net/toys/toylist1.html (viewed 2 November 2011).

14 H. van Dijk, *Twentieth-century Architecture in the Netherlands* (Rotterdam: 010 Publishers, 1999), p. 58.

15 Yves Saint Laurent, 1965 see http://www.metmuseum.org/toah/works-of-art/C.I.69.23 (viewed 2 November 2011).

16 http://www.ahalife.com/product/214/lego-purses/ (viewed 2 November 2011).

17 R. Padovan, *Towards Universality: Le Corbusier, Mies and De Stijl* (London: Routledge, 2002), p. 16.

18 B. Mulder and I. van Zijl, *Rietveld Schröder House* (New York: Princeton Architectural Press, 1999), p. 8.

19 J. van Eldonk and H. Fassbinder, *Flexible Fixation,* (Eindhoven: Assen: Van Gorcum; Eindhoven University of Technology, 1990), p. 12.

20 Padovan, *Towards Universality: Le Corbusier, Mies and De Stijl* p. 18.

21 H. Vera, 'On Dutch Windows', *Qualitative Sociology,* 12(2), 1989, pp. 215–34.

22 http://www.norwich.edu/voices/lisaschrenk/ page/4/ (viewed 2 November 2011).

23 J. Molema, *The New Modern Movement in the Netherlands 1924–1936* (Rotterdam: 010 Publishers, 1996), p. 80.

24 Netherlands Architecture Institute, *Living in the Lowlands 1850–2004* (Rotterdam: NAi Publishers, 2004), p. 12.

25 Ibid.

26 van Eldonk and Fassbinder, *Flexible Fixation,* pp. 22–24.

27 Ibid.

28 van Dijk, *Twentieth-century Architecture in the Netherlands,* p .134.

29 http://www.architectureguide.nl/project/ list_projects_of_architect/arc_id/717/prj_id/609

(viewed 2 November 2011).

30 van Eldonk and Fassbinder, *Flexible Fixation,* p. 15.

31 http://commons.wikimedia.org/wiki/ File:Rijksmuseum.Amsterdam.jpg (viewed 12 July 2012)

32 Padovan, *Towards Universality: Le Corbusier, Mies and De Stijl,* p. 156.

CHAPTER EIGHT: BAYKO AND SUBURBIA

1   http://www.theweeweb.co.uk/public/ladybird_authors.php?id=400 (viewed 6 September 2011).

2   A lot of the information presented here about Bayko comes from the admirable website 'Bayko by the Baykoman' at http://www.bayko.org.uk/ (viewed 6 September 2011). This site is a veritable Bayko encyclopedia.

3   Bayko (1934) *Book of Instructions* available at http://www.baykoman.com/Literature/1934%20 Early%20Sets%201%20to%205/jspw3_pop. htm?Page%25201.jpg,600,,txt%253Ci%253EBAY KO%253C/i%253E.%2520Manual%2520for%2 520the%2520Earliest%2520Sets%25201934%2 520Front%2520Cover,1.26,First1934FrontCover Earliest,1934%20Early%20Sets%201%20to%20 5,20,0,120,0,600,468,1,,..v_w_d_.._v_w_d_vwd_ scripts_v_w_d_ (viewed 11 October 2011).

4   http://www.bayko.org.uk/ (viewed 6 September 2011).

5   Bakelite Ltd 'A Happy Xmas Gift for Children' advertisement in *British Plastics and Moulded Products Trader*, December 1934, p. 208.

6   E. Lucas, *Light Buildings* (London: The Technical Press Ltd, 1935).

7   http://portal.acs.org/portal/acs/corg/ content?_nfpb=true&_pageLabel=PP_ ARTICLEMAIN&node id=924&content_ id=WPCP_007586&use_sec=true&sec_url_ var=region1&__uuid=fd35dcac-cbff-4651-8881-fbacd8e03e4b (viewed 6 September 2011).

8   http://www.birchvalley.co.uk/uploads/Non%20 shrink%20Paxolin%20and%20Matting.pdf (viewed 6 September 2011).

9   P. Randall, *The Products of Binns Road: A general survey* (Andover: Cavendish Books, 1981), p. 96.

10 P. Bradley, 'Bayko set sales', 15 July 2011 at http://www.bayko.org.uk/ (viewed 6 September 2011).

11 Canadian Logs were a Canadian toy much like Lincoln Logs and were manufactured from the 1930s to the 1970s. This information is taken from the very comprehensive Architoys website. See http://www.architoys.net/toys/toypages/canlogs. html (viewed 6 September 2011).

12 W. Rybczynski, *The Most Beautiful House in the World* (New York: Viking Penguin, 1989), p. 35.

13 Ibid., p. 34.

14 W. Rybczynski, *Looking Around: A journey through*

architecture, (New York: Viking, 1992), pp. 184–85.

15 *CIAM's The Athens Charter* (1933) Translated from the French by Anthony Eardley from Le Corbusier's *The Athens Charter* (New York: Grossman, 1973) at http://modernistarchitecture. wordpress.com/2010/11/03/ciam%E2%80%99s-%E2%80%9Cthe-athens-charter%E2%80%9 D-1933/ (viewed 11 October 2011).

16 E. Rubin, 'The Athens Charter' in *Themenportal Europäische Geschichte* (2009) at http://www.europa. clio-online.de/2009/Article=372 (viewed 11 October 2011).

17 E. Mumford, *The CIAM Discourse on Urbanism, 1928–1960* (Cambridge: The MIT Press, 2000), p. 9.

18 http://www.shipstamps.co.uk/forum/viewtopic. php?f=2&t=5748 (viewed 11 October 2011).

19 Mumford, *The CIAM Discourse on Urbanism, 1928–1960*, p. 77.

20 Ibid.

21 Rubin, *Themenportal Europäische Geschichte*.

22 A. Baillieu, 'Style: I want to play with the skyscraper', *The Independent*, 6 November 1993 at http://www.independent.co.uk/life-style/ fashion/news/style-i-want-to-play-with-the-skyscraper-an-exhibition-of-architectural-toys-in-london-is-stimulating-nostalgia-and-raising-establishment-eyebrows-says-amanda-baillieu-1502529.html (viewed 12 Oct 2011).

23 G. Binmore, 'Plus ça change' in 'Letters', *RIBA Journal*, May 2009, p. 32.

24 E. Blyton, *Noddy Goes to Toyland* (London: Sampson Low, 1949).

25 http://www.psfk.com/2012/02/ikea-prefab-houses.html (viewed 20 April 2012).

26 http://lambiek.net/artists/h/harmsen_van_beek. htm (viewed 12 October 2011).

27 J. M. Richards, *Castles on the ground* (London: The Architectural Press, 1946).

28 http://www.hsomerville.com/mwmailorder/ Bayko.htm (viewed 12 October 2011).

CHAPTER NINE: MINIBRIX AND UNASSUMING ARCHITECTURE

1 Anon, n.d., 'Minibrix' at http://www.museumof childhood.org.uk/collections/construction-toys/ minibrix/ (viewed 11 September 2011).

2 Gamages, *Gamages Christmas Toys and Games*, (Gamages: London, 1936), p. 11.

3 M. Lauwert, *The Place of Play: Toys and digital cultures* (Amsterdam: Amsterdam University Press, 2009), p. 52.

4 Hampshire Museums Service, 'Minibrix' (2011) at http://www3.hants.gov.uk/museum/childhood-collections/toys/minibrix.htm (viewed 11 September 2011).

5 http://www.powerhousemuseum.com/collection/ database/?irn=108980 (viewed 11 September 2011).

6 'The models and diagrams have been drawn up under the supervision of a leading architect, the late Mr. W.A.T. Carter, A.R.I.B.A.', as appears on the first page of all Minibrix instruction booklets.

7 F. Chatterton (ed.), *Who's Who in Architecture* (London: The Architectural Press, 1923), p. 49.

8 L. Weaver, *Small Country Houses: Their repair and enlargement: Forty examples chosen from five centuries* (London: Country life, 1914), pp. 197–99. The book gives the designer as W. T. A. Carter, but this seems an error as no such architect has been discovered.

9 W. A. T. Carter, *Architect and Building News* 165 (24 January 1941), p. 77.

10 http://www.petersfieldcam.co.uk/Forum/ viewtopic.php?f=5&t=76 (viewed 2 October 2011).

11 http://www.petersfieldcam.co.uk/Forum/view topic.php?f=5&t=400 (viewed 2 October 2011).

12 J. S. Skinner, *Form and Fancy: Factories and factory buildings by Wallis, Gilbert and Partner* (Liverpool: Liverpool University Press, 1997).

13 Pevsner said 'A bicycle shed is a building; Lincoln Cathedral is a piece of architecture'. N. Pevsner, *Outline of European Architecture* (Harmondsworth: Penguin Books, 1943), p. 15.

14 J. Summerson, 'Bread and Butter and Architecture', *The Architect and Building News* (25 December 1942), p. 193.

15 *The Times*, 27 July 1900, p. 10, col E.

16 Obituaries: Jean Savory, *The Telegraph*, 2 August 2000, at http://www.telegraph.co.uk/news/ obituaries/1351128/Jean-Savory.html (viewed 2 October 2011).

17 After leaving the LCC, Winmill's private practice mainly consisted of church work; an early design for a church when at the AA, praised by May as being exactly suited to its site: J. Summerson, *The Architectural Association 1847–1947* (London: Pleiades Books, 1947), Plate 16.

18 J. M. Winmill, *Charles Canning Winmill: An architect's life* (London: J. M. Dent and Sons, 1946), p. 43.

19 J.S Grosvenor, *A History of the Architecture of the UDSA Forest service* (1999) at http://www. foresthistory.org/ASPNET/Publications/ architecture/chap2a.htm (viewed 5 October 2011).

20 http://www.gpsmycity.com/tours/sheffield-museums-and-art-galleries-4453.html (viewed 5 October 2011).

21 A New London Fire Station, *The Times*, 9 January 1908, p. 9, col. A.

22 J. B. Nadal, *London's Fire Stations*, (Huddersfield: Jeremy Mills Publishing, 2006), p. 109.

23 http://www.sydenhamsociety.com/2010/11/a-history-of-perry-vale-fire-station/ (viewed 5 October 2011).

24 http://www.britishlistedbuildings.co.uk/en-

203396-fire-station-catford (viewed 5 October 2011).

25 Winmill, *Charles Canning Winmill: an Architect's Life*, p. 58.

26 J. Summerson, *The Unromantic Castle* (London: Thames & Hudson, 1990), p. 243.

27 http://www.britishlistedbuildings.co.uk/en-478645-belsize-fire-station-36-hampstead (viewed 5 October 2011).

28 M. Seaborne and R. Lowe, *The English School its architecture and organisation: Volume II 1870-1970* (London: Routledge and Kegan Paul, 1977), p. 86.

29 M. Seaborne, *The English School: Its architecture and organisation: Volume I 1370–1870* (London: Routledge and Kegan Paul, 1971), p. 131.

30 Ibid., p. 163.

31 N. R. Engelhardt, 'The Cost of School Buildings', *Review of Educational Research* 12(2), April 1942, p. 224.

32 C. Hubert and L. S. Shapiro, *William Lescaze* (New York: Institute for Architecture and Urban Studies and Rizzoli International Publications, 1982), p. 31.

33 A Central School was one for older children, and therefore positioned centrally in a district: F. Clay, *Modern School Buildings* 3rd edn (London: Batsford, 1929; first published 1902), p. 119.

34 J. A. Godfrey and R. C. Cleary, *School Design and Construction* (London: Architectural Press, 1953), p. 23.

35 Seaborne and Lowe, *The English School: Its architecture and organisation: Volume II 1870–1970*, pp. 86–87.

36 The wooden walls are still visible in a 1949 class photo taken outside, see http://www.sixtownships.org.uk/images/barringtonphotos/pages/barringtonprimaryschool1949_jpg.htm (viewed 5 October 2011).

37 http://www.dmm.org.uk/colliery/b035.htm (viewed 5 October 2011).

38 G. Topham Forrest, 'The modern school and the future race', *The Architects' Journal* 59, June 1924, p. 1014.

39 Seaborne and Lowe, *The English School: Its architecture and organisation: Volume II 1870–1970*, pp. 65–66.

40 M. Seaborne, *Primary School Design* (London: Routledge and Kegan Paul, 1971), p. 36.

41 F. Clay, *Modern School Buildings*, p. 117.

42 S. Taylor, *Modern Homesteads*, London: The Land Agents' Record Ltd, 1905), p. 7.

43 E. Gunn, *Life and Opinions* (Privately Published, 1953), pp. 61–62.

44 E. Gunn, *Farm Buildings: New and adapted* (London: Crosby Lockwood and Son, Ltd, 1935), p. 101.

45 E. Gunn, 'Events and Comments; The Builder Competition', *The Architect and Building News* (9 March 1951), p. 275.

46 See, for example, E. Gunn, *Little Things that Matter for Those who Build* (London: The Architectural Press, 1925) and E. Gunn, *Economy in House Design* (London: Architectural Press, 1932).

47 E. Gunn, 'Piggeries and Poultry Houses: Accommodation on housing estates', *The Builder* 157 (24 November 1939), pp. 737–38.

48 Gunn, *Little Things that Matter for Those who Build*, p. 71.

49 Gunn, *Life and Opinions*, p. 86.

CHAPTER TEN: JUNEERO AND THE ARCHITECTURE OF MAKE-DO-AND-MEND

1 C. Ungewitter (ed.), L. A. Ferry (transl.) and G. Haim (transl.), *Science and Salvage* (London: The Scientific Book Club, 1946) p. 99. The original German book was published in 1938.

2 http://bc150.ecuad.ca/museum/09_06.html (viewed 14 November 2011).

3 http://www.nzmeccano.com/image-54725 (viewed 10 March 2012).

4 Ministry of Home Security, *Air Raids: What you must know, what you must do* (London: HMSO, 1940) pp. 17–18

5 Tecton Architects, *Planned A.R.P.* (London: The Architectural Press, 1939) p. 35.

6 Ibid., p. 135.

7 P. Lewis, *A People's War* (London: Methuen, 1986) p. 75.

8 Civil Defence, *Some Things You should know if War should come: Public Information Leaflet No. 1* (London: Lord Privy Seal's Office, July 1939).

9 C. W. Glover, *Civil Defence* 2nd edn (London: Chapman and Hall, Ltd, 1940) pp. 321–25.

10 S. Giedion, *Mechanization Takes Command* (New York: Oxford University Press, 1948), p. 436.

11 The Morrison Shelter was designed by John (later Baron) Baker using the new plastic theory of steel structural behaviour, developed by Baker, who was later to be the head of the Engineering School at Cambridge University.

12 http://collections.vam.ac.uk/item/O37227/construction-kit-juneero-no-1-set/ (viewed 10 March 2012).

13 http://www.tankmuseum.org/ (viewed 10 March 2012.)

14 http://www.nzmeccano.com/image-54567 (viewed 10 March 2012.)

15 See, for example, S. Wigglesworth *9/10 Stock Orchard Street – fact file & credits* (London: Sarah Wigglesworth Architects, undated).

16 R .J. Cole and P. C. Kernan 'Life-cycle Energy Use in Office Buildings', *Building and Environment*, 31(4), 1996, pp. 307–17.

17 B. Braithwaite, N. Walsh and G. Davies, *The Home Front: The best of Good Housekeeping 1939–1945* (London: Leopard Books, 1995), p. 162.

18 http://www.nzmeccano.com/image-54724

(viewed 2 April 2012).

19 http://www.nzmeccano.com/image-54725 (viewed 2 April 2012).

20 S. O. Shapiro *O Tempora! O Mores!: Cicero's Catilinarian Orations: a Student Edition with Historical Essays* (Norman, OK: University of Oklahoma Press, 2005).

CHAPTER ELEVEN: CASTOS AND CONCRETE ON THE CARPET

1 1947 is the date given in the entry for Castos at http://www.architoys.net/toys/toylist1.html (viewed 13 October 2011).

2 Castos, *Basic Building Yard* (Hadley, Salop: Castos Ltd, undated, assumed 1947).

3 Connolly J. G. Pty Ltd 'Boys – Here is a Fascinating New Hobby', *Hobbies Illustrated*, November 1948, p. 146.

4 Connolly J.G. Pty Ltd, 'Special Offer to Model Railwaymen', *Hobbies Illustrated*, November 1949, p. 121.

5 D. Yeomans and D. Cottam, *Owen Williams*, (London: RIBA Publications, 2001).

6 Maurlyn Manufacturing Pty Ltd, 'Right on Time!', *Hobbies Illustrated*, November 1948, p. 173.

7 http://www.rbnz.govt.nz/statistics/0135595.html (viewed 13 October 2011).

8 See, for example, F. R. S. Yorke, *The Modern House* (Cheam, Surrey: The Architectural Press, 1943), p. 10.

9 R. Taylor, *Roman Builders: A study in architectural process* (Cambridge: Cambridge University Press, 2003), p. 8.

10 http://www.romanconcrete.com/index.htm (viewed 13 October 2011)

11 D. Moore. 'The Pantheon: Crown jewel of roman concrete', *Constructor*, September 2002, pp. 22–26.

12 http://www.concretecontractor.com/concrete-history/ (viewed 13 October 2011).

13 History Detectives, *Episode 1, 2004 – Edison House, Union, New Jersey* (Public Broadcasting Service, 2004) at http://www-tc.pbs.org/opb/historydetectives/static/media/transcripts/2011-05-24/201_edison.pdf (viewed 26 October 2011).

14 http://www.phippsny.org/about_history.html (viewed 1 November 2011).

15 IEEE *Concrete Housing* (IEEE Global History Network, 2011) at http://www.ieeeghn.org/wiki/index.php/Concrete_Housing (viewed 25 October 2011).

16 See photograph '*Construction of a cement house in Union, NJ, 1919. Courtesy: National Park Service, Edison National Historic Site*' at http://www.ieeeghn.org/wiki/index.php/File:Concrete_Housing.jpg (viewed 1 November 2011).

17 R. Whiteread, J. Lingwood and J. Bird, *House* (London: Phaidon, 1995).

18 http://www.cement.org/basics/concreteproducts_tilt.asp (viewed 1 November 2011).

19 M. Johnson, 'Tilt-up pioneer: Robert Aiken developed tilt-up construction nearly 100 years ago', *Concrete Construction*, August 2002, at http://findarticles.com/p/articles/mi_m0NSX/is_8_47/ai_91086855/?tag=content;col1 (viewed 1 November 2011).

20 H. R. Arkes and P. Ayton, 'The Sunk Cost and Concorde effects: Are humans less rational than lower animals?', *Psychological Bulletin*, 125(5), September 1999, pp. 591–600.

21 'Tilt-up Construction: History and Uses' at http://www.concretecontractor.com/tilt-up-concrete/construction-history/ (viewed 1 November 2011).

22 Castos, *Castos: Links hand and brain in creative pleasure* (Hadley, Salop: Castos Ltd, n.d., assumed 1947), p. 3.

23 Ibid.

24 Ibid.

25 S. Pepper and P. Richmond, 'Reilly, Sir Charles Herbert (1874–1948)', *Oxford Dictionary of National Biography* (Oxford: Oxford University Press, 2004) at http://www.oxforddnb.com/view/article/35721 (viewed 10 November 2011).

26 B. Guise and P. Brook, *The Midland Hotel: Morecambe's white hope* (Lancaster: Palatine Books, 2009).

27 Havering London Borough, '64 Heath Drive, Gidea Park', *Listed Buildings Register* at http://www.havering.gov.uk/Pages/HeathDriveGideaPark-LGSL-514.aspx (viewed 11 November 2011).

28 J. Siers, *The Life and Times of James Walter Chapman-Taylor* (Napier: Millwood Heritage Productions, 2007).

29 http://www.linkaworld.com (viewed 28 May 2012)

CHAPTER TWELVE: BILT-E-Z, GIRDER AND PANEL, ARKITEX AND THE BRAVE NEW WORLD

1 R. Herz-Fischler, *The Shape of the Great Pyramid*, (Waterloo: Wifrid Laurier University Press, 2000), pp. 10–16.

2 *The Holy Bible*, King James version, Genesis 11:1–9

3 http://en.wikipedia.org/wiki/Iron_Pagoda (viewed 18 November 2011).

4 http://www.sacred-destinations.com/england/lincoln-cathedral (viewed 18 November 2011).

5 http://en.wikipedia.org/wiki/Monadnock_Building (viewed 18 November 2011).

6 http://www.architoys.net/toys/toylist1.html (viewed 18 November 2011).

7 Anon., 'Real Toys for Real Boys', *Pittsburgh Press*, 14 December 1927, p. 33 at http://news.google.com/newspapers?nid=1144&dat=19271214&

id=kzkbAAAAIBAJ&sjid=O0oEAAAAIBAJ&
pg=5642,5513671 (viewed 20 February 2012).

8 G. Cousins and P. Maximuke, 'Detroit's Last
Depot, Part 2: The Ceremony was 61 Years Late',
Trains Magazine, August 1978, pp. 40–48.

9 http://www.nbm.org/exhibitions-collections/
collections/toy-collection.html (viewed 20
February 2012).

10 For example, 'King's Dream of New York', Harry
M. Pettit (illustrator), *King's Views of New York*
(New York: Moses King, 1908), frontispiece.

11 All information from http://www.girderpanel.
com/ (viewed 18 November 2011).

12 http://en.wikipedia.org/wiki/Girder_and_Panel_
building_sets (viewed 18 November 2011).

13 1956 Trans Canada Bridge and Pam 'n' Andy
Structural Building Sets manufactured by Peter-
Austin Manufacturing Co., Toronto, Ontario
Canada described at http://www.girderpanel.com

14 http://www.tcawestern.org/lionel.htm (viewed 20
February 2012).

15 http://www.lionel.com/CentralStation/
LionelPastAndPresent/ (viewed 20 February
2012).

16 http://www.tcawestern.org/af.htm (viewed 20
February 2012).

17 For a detailed overview of Marx trains see http://
www.toyandtrainguides.com/marxtin.htm (viewed
20 February 2012).

18 'Alan Arnold's Train Set' in the 'Hall of Fame' at
http://www.girderpanel.com/ (viewed 23 March
2012).

19 http://www.architoys.net/toys/toypages/arkitex.
html (viewed 18 November 2011).

20 http://www.tri-angrailways.org.uk/arkitex3.htm;
http://www.tri-angrailways.org.uk/arkitex4.htm
(viewed 11 November 2011).

21 J. Day. *Tri-ang Arkitex Construction System (00/H0
Series) Set Contents & Components* (2000) at http://
www.architoys.net/toys/toypages/arkitex00.html
(viewed 20 February 2012).

22 Ibid.

23 http://www.btmbeijing.com/contents/
en/business/2004-05/focus/soho (viewed
20 February 2012).

24 J. Glancey, 'The miniature world of Olivo
Barbieri', *The Guardian*, 17 February 2006.

**CHAPTER THIRTEEN: PLAYPLAX AND
DECONSTRUCTION**

1 http://www.playplax.co.uk/3/about-playplax
(viewed 26 January 2012).

2 Anon., 'Duke of Edinburgh's Prize for Elegant
Design: Patrick Ryland for Trendon toys', *Design
Journal* 258, 1970, p. 34.

3 http://www.retrowow.co.uk/retro_britain/
toys_and_games/playplax.php (viewed 26 January
2012).

4 Anon., 'Duke of Edinburgh's Prize for Elegant
Design: Patrick Ryland for Trendon toys', *Design
Journal* 258, 1970, p. 34.

5 http://www.designcouncil.org.uk/about-us/
Prince-Philip-Designers-Prize/19691978/
(viewed 26 January 2012).

6 http://projectswordtoys.blogspot.com/2010/09/
through-glass-clearly.html (viewed 26 January
2012).

7 http://www.kengarland.co.uk/KGA%20
graphic%20design/galt%20toys/index.html
(viewed 26 January 2012).

8 http://www.virtualtoychest.com/playplax/
playplax.html (viewed 26 January 2012).

9 I. Bars and J. Terning, *Extra Dimensions in Space and
Time* (New York: Springer, 2010), pp. 59–63.

10 A. Clark, 'Playplax is a Star Performer for
Wheatley Plastics', 6 December 2011, at
http://www.prw.com/subscriber/headlines2.
html?cat=1&id=146 (viewed 26 January 2012).

11 http://menmedia.co.uk/manchestereveningnews/
news/business/enterprise/s/1466994_wheatley-
plastics-produces-playplax-toy-for-portobello-
games (viewed 26 January 2012).

12 P. Scheerbart and B. Taut in D. Sharp (ed.), *Glass
Architecture and Alpine Architecture* (New York:
Praeger, 1972).

13 P. Johnson and M. Wigley, *Deconstructivist
Architecture*, (New York: Museum of Modern Art,
1988) p. 11.

14 http://blog.blagman.co.uk/2011/06/play-plax.
html (viewed 5 March 2012).

15 http://uk.tourisme93.com/document.
php?pagendx=10015 (viewed 2 February 2012).

16 Manet painted *A Bar at the Folies-Bergère* in 1882,
just before his death.

17 M. Wigley, *The Architecture of Deconstruction:
Derrida's Haunt* (Cambridge, Massachusetts: The
MIT Press, 1993), p. xi.

18 http://behnisch.com/projects/459 (viewed
13 February 2012).

19 D. Libeskind and P. Goldberg, *Counterpoint: Daniel
Libeskind in conversation with Paul Goldberg* (New
York: The Monacelli Press, 2008), p. 202.

20 Ibid., pp. 206-7.

21 http://www.chinadaily.com.cn/
china/2009-02/10/content_7461514.htm (viewed
13 February 2012).

22 N. Leach in N. Ray (ed.) *Architecture and its Ethical
Dilemmas*, (Abingdon: Taylor and Francis, 2005)
pp. 141–42.

23 http://madhousefamilyreviews.blogspot.
co.nz/2011/10/playplax-review.html (viewed
13 February 2012.

CHAPTER FOURTEEN: LEGO AND THE GREEN CITY

1 J. Pisani, 'The Making of…a LEGO', *After Work* 29 November 2006, at http://www.businessweek. com/bwdaily/dnflash/content/nov2006/db2006 1127_153826.htm (viewed 16 February 2012).

2 http://www.minibrix.com/history.html (viewed 16 February 2012).

3 http://www.flickr.com/photos/27742455@ N06/3250104502/in/photostream/ (viewed 16 February 2012).

4 http://www.toyhistory.com/Halsam.html (viewed 16 February 2012).

5 http://reviews.ebay.com/Halsam-American-Plastic-Bricks-by-Elgo-A-Guide?ugid= 10000000002067096 (viewed 16 February 2012).

6 http://www.toyhistory.com/Halsam.html (viewed 16 February 2012).

7 http://plastics.americanchemistry.com/Life-Cycle (viewed 16 February 2012).

8 http://www.architoys.net/toys/toypages/ ambricks.html (viewed 16 February 2012).

9 http://reviews.ebay.com/Halsam-American -Plastic-Bricks-by-Elgo-A-Guide?ugid= 10000000002067096 (viewed 16 February 2012).

10 These can be seen on the cover on the American Plastic Bricks manual at Raymond Howard's Flickr site, which contains many interesting and useful photographs and scans: http://www.flickr. com/photos/27742455@N06/2780442462/in/ photostream/ (viewed 17 February 2012).

11 http://www.balmoralsoftware.com/apb/ halsamparts.jpg (viewed 17 February 2012).

12 http://www.toyhistory.com/Halsam.html (viewed 17 February 2012).

13 http://www.balmoralsoftware.com/apb/elgoparts. jpg (viewed 17 February 2012).

14 We have no evidence for this other than the sets themselves; the New Zealand one has a sad little erratum slip which says that due to a misprint, 'metal strips' in the instruction manual should read 'cardboard strips.'

15 J. Sbriglio, *L'Unité d'habitation de Marseille/the Unité d'habitation in Marseilles* (Basel: Fondation Le Corbusier/Birkhäuser, 2004) p. 113.

16 We do not have a set of American Skyline, and the only one we have seen was in the National Building Museum in Washington D.C., where photographs are not permitted.

17 http://www.hilarypagetoys.com/history.php?his_ id=4 (viewed 6 February 2012)

18 H. F. Page, 'Plastics as a Medium for Toys.' *Daily Graphic Plastics Exhibition Catalogue* 1946, pp.112–14.

19 J. Hughes and C. Saunter, *Hilary Fisher Page and Kiddicraft*, 11 May 2008, at http://www. hilarypagetoys.com/history.php?his_id=4 (viewed 6 February 2012).

20 The Patent Office, 'Improvements in Toy Building Bricks', *Patent Specification 587,206*, (London: HMSO, 1947).

21 Hughes and Saunter, *Hilary Fisher Page and Kiddicraft*. Page's suicide is mentioned in a letter from Sir Robin Jacob, quoted in J. Phillips, 'LEGO- a great British invention', 24 December 2011, on the IPKaT copyright and patent blog at http://ipkitten.blogspot.co.nz/2011/12/lego-great-british-invention.html (viewed 16 February 2012).

22 C. Lewis and C. Short, *A Latin Dictionary: Founded on Andrews' edition of Freund's Latin dictionary* (Oxford: Clarendon Press, 1879).

23 Hughes and Saunter, *Hilary Fisher Page and Kiddicraft*.

24 See image at http://brickfetish.com/ sets/700/700_3_1950.html (viewed 16 February 2012). Anyone wanting to study the history of Lego needs to visit Jim Hughes's Brickfetish website, which is a veritable Lego encyclopedia.

25 Interlego A.G v Tyco Industries Inc. & Ors (Hong Kong) [1988] UKPC 3 (5 May 1988) Privy Council Appeal No. 43 of 1987 Date: Delivered 5 May 1988.

26 http://www.architoys.net/toys/toypages/bettabil. html (viewed 17 February 2012).

27 See, for example, http://skuds.org/2012/01/ betta-bilda/ and a message at http://talktalk. myfreeforum.org/index.php?component=content &topicid=1816 (viewed 17 February 2012).

28 J. Phillips, 'An Empire Built of Bricks: A brief appraisal of Lego', *European Intellectual Property Review* 12, 1987, pp. 363–66.

29 Interlego A.G v Tyco Industries Inc. & Ors (Hong Kong) [1988] UKPC 3 (05 May 1988) Privy Council Appeal No. 43 of 1987 Date: Delivered 5 May 1988.

30 http://brickfetish.com/timeline/1958.html (viewed 17 February 2012).

31 Ibid.

32 Ibid.

33 http://www.stevenage.gov.uk/about-stevenage/ museum/47012/46962/47008/ (viewed 17 February 2012).

34 A. Alexander, *Britain's New Towns: Garden Cities to Sustainable Communities* (Abingdon: Routledge, 2009), p. 54.

35 Economist Intelligence Unit, *European Green City Index: Assessing the environmental impact of Europe's major cities* (Munich: Siemens, AG, 2009), p. 6.

36 Ibid., p. 8.

37 Ibid., p. 33.

38 The LEGO Group, *Progress Report 2011* (Billund, Denmark: The LEGO Group, 2011), p. 14.

39 Economist Intelligence Unit, *European Green City Index: Assessing the environmental impact of Europe's major cities*, p. 10.

40 Green Party of Aotearoa New Zealand, 'Building

for sustainable transport, healthier communities, and individual well being' in *Housing Policy – Living Well* (2012) at http://www.greens.org.nz/sites/default/files/housingpolicy.pdf (viewed 20 February 2012).

41 http://www.plasticseurope.org/what-is-plastic/types-of-plastics/abssan/how-are-abs-and-san-madeand-processed.aspx (viewed 20 February 2012).

42 The LEGO Group, *Progress Report*, p. 45.

43 http://upmplastic.com/Cornstarch_degradable_epi_oxo_technical2.asp (viewed 20 February 2012).

44 http://epp.eurostat.ec.europa.eu/statistics_explained/index.php/Glossary:Kilograms_of_oil_equivalent_(kgoe) (viewed 20 February 2012).

45 R. Vale and B. Vale, *Time to Eat the Dog? The real guide to sustainable living* (London: Thames and Hudson, 2009), p. 77.

46 R. Bryce, 'Gas pains', *Atlantic Magazine,* May 2005, at http://www.theatlantic.com/magazine/archive/2005/05/gas-pains/3897/ and http://www.mitenergyclub.org/assets/2008/11/15/Units_ConvFactors.MIT_EnergyClub_Factsheet.v8.pdf (both viewed 20 February 2012).

47 B. Vale and R. Vale, *The New Autonomous House* (London: Thames and Hudson, 2000).

48 OECD Environment Directorate, *OECD Key Environmental Indicators* (Paris: OECD, 2008), p. 19.

49 K. Ravilious, 'How green is your pet?' *New Scientist* 2731, 23 October 2009, pp. 46–47. This is based on Vale and Vale, *Time to Eat the Dog? The real guide to sustainable living.*

50 See, for example, the following series of papers: A. Atkinson, 'Cities after oil—1: "Sustainable development" and energy futures', *City* 11(2), 2007, pp. 201–13; A. Atkinson, 'Cities after oil—2: Background to the collapse of "modern" civilisation', *City* 11(3), 2007, pp. 293–312; A. Atkinson, 'Cities after oil—3: Collapse and the fate of cities', *City* 11(2), 2008, pp. 201–13; A. Atkinson, 'Cities after oil (one more time)', *City* 13(4), 2009, pp. 493–98.

CHAPTER FIFTEEN: LEARNING ARCHITECTURE ON THE CARPET

1 Meccano Ltd, '8.23 Lifeboat and Tractor', *Instructions for No. 7 and 8 Outfits* (Liverpool: Meccano Ltd, 1947), pp. 55–56.

Picture Credits

28 Judith Cantell. 35 Malcolm Hanson. 82 (above and below) Norwegian University of Science and Technology. 94 (below) Judith Cantell. 95 (above and below) Maarten Gehem. 97 Photograph by Beatriz Busaniche; used under Wikimedia Creative Commons Licence 3.0 http://creativecommons.org/licenses/by-sa/3.0/deed.en. Location of image http://commons.wikimedia.org/wiki/File:Rijksmuseum.Amsterdam.jpg. 122 Beamish, The Living Museum of the North. 170 Photograph by Ra Boe; used under Wikimedia Creative Commons Licence 3.0 http://creativecommons.org/licenses/by-sa/3.0/de/legalcode. Location of image http://commons.wikimedia.org/wiki/File:Stuttgart_Uni_Vaihingen_campus_04.jpg. 171 photograph by Paul Hermans; used under Wikimedia Creative Commons Licence 2.5 http://creativecommons.org/licenses/by-sa/2.5/deed.en; Location of image http://commons.wikimedia.org/wiki/File:Manchester_Imperial_War_Museum_North_17-10-2009_16-34-57.jpg. 182 Jim Hughes.

The authors would also like to thank Paul Hillier of Victoria University of Wellington who did all the scans of original sources and the pictures of box lids.

Acknowledgments

We would like to thank very much the following people and organisations who have helped us in the creation of this book. The errors, however, are all our own.

Beamish, the Living Museum of the North
Stan Baker (Wellington Meccano Club)
Judith Cantell
Tobias Danielmeyer (Victoria University of Wellington)
Maarten Gehem
Malcolm Hanson
Paul Hillier (Victoria University of Wellington)
Jim Hughes
Paul James
Pauline Reid (The National Trust of Australia)
Irene Schamper
Yvonne Shaw
Marit Støren Valen (Norwegian University of Science and Technology)

Index

206